CRYPTO CROWDS

Critical Interventions: A Forum for Social Analysis
General Editor: Bruce Kapferer

Volume 21
CRYPTO CROWDS
Singularities and Multiplicities on the Blockchain
Edited by Matan Shapiro

Volume 20
EXTREMISM, SOCIETY, AND THE STATE
Edited by Giacomo Loperfido

Volume 19
WHO'S CASHING IN?
Contemporary Perspectives on New Monies and Global Cashlessness
Edited by Atreyee Sen, Johan Lindquist and Marie Kolling

Volume 18
DEMOCRACY'S PARADOX
Populism and its Contemporary Crisis
Edited by Bruce Kapferer and Dimitrios Theodossopoulos

Volume 17
THE GLOBAL LIFE OF AUSTERITY
Comparing Beyond Europe
Edited by Theodoros Rakopolous

Volume 16
MORAL ANTHROPOLOGY
A Critique
Edited by Bruce Kapferer and Marina Gold

Volume 15
THE EVENT OF *CHARLIE HEBDO*
Imaginaries of Freedom and Control
Edited by Alessandro Zagato

Volume 14
ARAB SPRING
Uprisings, Powers, Interventions
Edited by Kjetil Fosshagen

Volume 13
WAR, TECHNOLOGY, ANTHROPOLOGY
Edited by Koen Stroeken

Volume 12
MIGRATION, DEVELOPMENT, AND TRANSNATIONALIZATION
A Critical Stance
Edited by Nina Glick Schiller and Thomas Faist

For a full volume listing, please see the series page on our website:

https://berghahnbooks.com/series/critical-interventions

CRYPTO CROWDS
Singularities and Multiplicities on the Blockchain

Edited by

Matan Shapiro

Paperback edition first published in 2024 by
Berghahn Books
www.berghahnbooks.com

© 2024 Matan Shapiro

All rights reserved.
Except for the quotation of short passages for the purposes
of criticism and review, no part of this book may be reproduced
in any form or by any means, electronic or mechanical,
including photocopying, recording, or any information
storage and retrieval system now known or to be invented,
without written permission of the publisher.

Library of Congress Cataloging-in-Publication Data

A C.I.P. catalogue record for this book is available from
the Library of Congress. Library of Congress Cataloging in
Publication Control Number: 2023050994

British Library Cataloguing in Publication Data

A catalogue record for this book is
available from the British Library.

ISBN 978-1-80539-292-7 paperback
ISBN 978-1-80539-293-4 epub
ISBN 978-1-80539-294-1 web pdf

https://doi.org/10.3167/9781805392927

The electronic open access publication of *Crypto Crowds*,
edited by Matan Shapiro has been made possible through the
generous financial support of Bergen University and the Norwegian
Research Council.

This work is published subject to a Creative Commons Attribution
Noncommercial No Derivatives 4.0 International license. The terms
of the license can be found at https://creativecommons.org/licenses/
by-nc-nd/4.0/. For permission to publish commercial volumes, contact
Berghahn Books.

This book is dedicated to Hanna,
Whose singularity cannot be multiplied

Contents

Introduction
Matan Shapiro
1

Towards Hyperbitcoinization
Bitcoin Maximalism as Speculative Fiction
Bruno Campos Cardoso
23

The Sociality of the Blockchain and
the Appification of Money
Affordances of a New Paradigm for Crowds
Dimitrios Tsavelis
40

Gambling Crowds as Crypto-oracles?
Bridging the Real and the Blockchain through
Utopian Markets and Oracular Shenanigans
Anthony J. Pickles
66

Affective Processes in Cryptocurrency Markets
An Exploration with Crowd Theory
Anna Vennonen
84

Unstructured Simplicity
The Peer-to-Peer Collective and
Concurrent Formations of Cryptocommunities
Mitchell Tuddenham
111

Conclusion
Matan Shapiro
134

Introduction

Matan Shapiro

The Analytic Curiosity

Trade in cryptocurrencies has given rise in the last decade to a fascinating analytic curiosity. On the one hand, wild cycles of boom-and-bust consolidated multiple buyers and sellers at a global scale. The emotional intensity that these commercial dynamics inspired – combining anticipation, thrill and gloom – translated empirically into such concepts as FOMO (Fear of Missing Out), FUD (Fear, Uncertainty and Doubt) or Alpha (outperforming markets), which themselves quickly became powerful discursive tools capable of directing and structuring value fluctuations or other relevant online trends. Calculations of gain and loss at the individual level thus interconnected millions of loosely related people around the world. Boom-and-bust cycles instigated in that sense an online crowding phenomenon, which dynamically brought multitudes into virtual convergence on trading platforms and forums.

On the other hand, however, ownership of cryptocurrencies and related assets have also given rise in the last few years to self-described 'coin-communities'. Such groups began organizing their own trading platforms on designated messaging apps, hold numerous meetups, attend lectures and conferences, or socialize during drinking nights. At the local level cryptocommunities often developed a unique slang and threw parties to celebrate both national and crypto-related holidays (e.g. 'The Pizza Day', which commemorates the first time Bitcoin was used to purchase real-world goods in 2010). Participation in these communities included ongoing ideological discussions on the scope of financial decentralization and on the algorithmic automation of trust, both of which are still considered to be key concepts in the world of crypto that also expose a certain millenarian dimension (cf. Faustino et al. 2022).

The 'curious' analytical point is that these dynamics are contradictory: the crowd, which in the context of digital sociality is composed of millions of unrelated individuals, tends to expand as it attracts more members (Canetti 1984 [1961]), while the community tends to enclose itself within concrete symbolic and semantic boundaries. Going beyond the ideological individualism that has often been depicted as the holy grail of crypto-economics (Golumbia 2016), this focus on the dynamic of collective phenomena opens up new ways to think of the sociality surrounding cryptocurrency and blockchain technology more generally. This collected volume includes ethnographic essays that experiment with this direction.

Cyberculture and the Communalist Ideal

New technologies, as Benedict Anderson (2016 [1983]) famously argued, can become catalysts for iconoclastic ideas, along with the revisionist social structures they advocate. The large-scale dissemination of newspapers and commercial novels across vast territories, for example, contributed to the construction of an 'imagined' unity between people who live far from one another. Machines that print en masse in different languages thus became pivotal to the eighteenth- and nineteenth-century emergence of nationalism, first in the Americas, then in the Caribbeans and finally in Europe. Anderson sought to deconstruct the widespread modern assumption that nationalism originates in ethnic essentialism and ancient traditions, or that nationalist sentiments can 'revive' the primordial sameness of a lingual community. Anderson's critique in fact goes beyond nationalism to highlight the critical yet entirely unintentional role of technological innovation in the transformation of dominant social discourses. He convincingly shows that new organizational and ideational formations emerge as part of the mundane adaptation of innovative technologies to existing social values, while simultaneously (and accidentally) also triggering the modification of these same values.

Fred Turner's (2006) work on Silicon Valley 'cyberculture' illustrates how a similar process took place in the United States due to the mass adoption of computation technologies (cf. Delanty 2003: 170). Turner shows that although liberal Americans in the 1960s saw computers as oppressing machines used by 'the military-industrial complex' to wage 'mechanistic' wars (Turner 2006: 12), by the 1980s computers were given quasi-magical properties as tools for personal and collective liberation (ibid, 14–16). Proponents of this approach thus began describing computers as vectors of connectivity and identified 'cyberspace' as a new frontier whose conquest will emancipate the human spirit (viz. Barlow 1996). Cyberculture pioneers' use of personal computers helped disseminate the imaginary of disembodied equality in cyberspace; which encouraged early adopters to see themselves as a spiritual avant-garde in the 'creation of the electronic agora ... [that is the] first step toward the implementation of direct democracy within all social institutions' (Barbrook and Cameron 1996: 48).

Turner focuses his analysis on the 'New Communalist' branch of the counterculture movement in the United

States, which at the end of the 1960s and the early 1970s set out to the woods to establish new communal settlements. Disappointed with the decadent technocracy they associated with middle-class livelihood – while equally disillusioned by the failure of the hippie movement to transform cultural and political priorities – communalists sought to advance egalitarian values, encourage the metaphysical enhancement of consciousness in the search for a meaningful existence, and promote ecological harmony. To live these values as mundane realities, they began to advocate small-scale DIY materialism, which enabled them to practise sustainability and self-reliance. As opposed to mainstream countercultural trends, which highlighted political action and society-scale reform (e.g. the Civil Rights Movement and the opposition to the war in Vietnam), the New Communalists retired to the margins of society to create their aspired utopias of democratic self-governance and spiritual holism.

Turner insists that these experiments were not heroic, forgotten, 'last stand' resorts in face of the globalization of commodities and labour or the expansion of corporate powers that radically transformed the global economy during and especially after the end of the Cold War. Rather, communalist inventions, ideas and values effectively merged into and even inspired the distributed form of American capitalism, becoming one of its most powerful ideological driving forces. More concretely, ideas about the humanity-scale liberating-potential of cybernetic systems, horizontal social relations as a vector for increased productivity, networked organization as the expression of equality and an emphasis on informal corporate culture have all come to define Silicon Valley entrepreneurial revisionism, which in the 2020s remains one of the most dominant business models for hi-tech and related industries the world over.

Barbrook and Cameron (1996) have argued convincingly that the success of this business model during the 1980s and 1990s could only take place due to the adoption of a lifestyle approach that they called the 'Californian Ideology', a somewhat paradoxical fusion between *reactionary* hippie ideas about communal solidarity and *radical* liberal-economic ideas about private wealth. Like other countercultural trends – such as the commercialization of recreational drugs, which were seen as tools for the expansion of individual and collective minds – the Californian Ideology fused anarcho-libertarian free market initiatives, which ideally lacked any regulation at all, with normative financial hierarchies (especially the corporate structure). Barbrook and Cameron write:

> Crucially, anti-statism provides the means to reconcile radical and reactionary ideas about technological progress. While the New Left resents the government for funding the military-industrial complex, the New Right attacks the state for interfering with the spontaneous dissemination of new technologies by market competition. Despite the central role played by public intervention in developing hypermedia [such as the nascent internet and later smartphones], the Californian ideologues preach an anti-statist gospel of hi-tech libertarianism: a bizarre mishmash of hippie anarchism and economic liberalism beefed up with lots of technological determinism. (1996: 57)

Although other processes were at play, the 'bizarre' emergence of a communalist-libertarian ideology in the 1980s and 1990s established the discursive grounds for the techno-utopian subcultures of the 2000s. The root metaphor of 'making the world a better place', a battered cliché by the 2020s, turned into self-aggrandizing mantra, which coated aggressive market-making strategies with quasi-religious universalist rhetoric. Californian techno-prophets indeed promoted new forms of personal freedoms and advocated individual expression, but they also highlighted the role of transnational 'communities' in the establishment of global citizenship. The idea of a universal civil society, emerging through the expansion of capital, had a collectivizing effect as much as it atomized the search for 'liberty'. Contemporary cryptocurrency adopters, who often highlight their membership in 'coin communities' (Swartz 2020: 2), increasingly apply this discourse to blockchain technology.

Blockchain Communities

Blockchain is a digital ledger that surfaced in 2008 as the operating system of Bitcoin, the first cryptocurrency. It was innovative for two main reasons. First, a blockchain system utilizes tamper-proof encryption techniques to produce money. It thus overrides the power of any single entity to control or manipulate data, while 'decentralizing' the process of accounting to a network of users. Second, the blockchain enables users to send and receive digital cash online without the mediation of 'trusted third parties' (Nakamoto 2008). This is possible because all participants hold a copy of the entire history of transactions and monitor each other in real time. Supporters call this 'trustlessness' (Buterin 2015b), meaning that users are not required to trust human decision making to verify that their transaction went through (Greenfield 2018; Faria 2019). Inscribed into the automatic function of algorithms, 'trustlessness' and decentralization thus made it possible to sustain direct relations between stakeholders in ways that circumvent the auditing power of state and tax authorities (Maurer 2016).

From its inception, the blockchain appealed to two types of supporters. First, given its decentralized modus operandi, it attracted libertarian advocates of free-market economic theories (Hayek 1980 [1948]). These people promoted the establishment of unregulated, extrastatist markets, premised on private initiative and micro-economic incentives. Second, due to its 'trustless' functionality, the blockchain attracted cypherpunks (Hayes 2019), who since the 1980s promoted the widespread use of encryption technologies to increase anonymity online. In both cases, early adopters hoped to use technology as a substitute to governmental regulation. Scholars in the social and human sciences were thus quick to realize that the blockchain was not a 'neutral' technology (Zimmer 2017), but rather an instrumental platform that has initially been built with the explicit ideological intention to articulate libertarian political-economic and philosophical values (Golumbia 2016).

The bulk of studies on the subject focused predominantly on the materiality of the new forms of digital money enabled by the blockchain and the kinds of new political-economic power structures it conjures (e.g. Golumbia 2016; Dodd 2018; Swartz 2018; Faria 2019). Scholars pointed out that techno-geeks, die-hard libertarians, and cybercriminals might not have much in common, but each developed their own subcultural styles of cryptocurrency use (Maddox et al. 2016). This reflected accurately nonacademic publications. Early adopters and supporters in fact stressed right from the beginning that they made part of a growing global movement whose members were not disconnected from each other. They mainly communicated on social media platforms, chat apps and Reddit forums, but since the early 2010s main activists and 'evangelists' also began meeting regularly in bars, cafes, conferences and cryptotrading rooms around the world. In these venues they advocated 'cryptonomics' (Buterin 2017) as a potential 'counterpower' (Scott 2014) to contemporary hegemonic forms of surveillance capitalism (Zuboff 2019), arguing that decentralized money is not merely a new technological innovation, but also a tool whose mass adoption will necessarily disrupt cultural norms and legal traditions that still endow established economic institutions with widespread social legitimacy.

As early as 2012–13, some cryptocurrency adopters thus began converging into 'coin communities' on- and offline (Popper 2015). Dogecoin, a decentralized digital currency created as a joke by Billy Markus and Jackson Palmer in 2013, is a prominent example. Markus and Palmer initially sought to ridicule the emergent cryptocurrency market and thus saw their coin as a passing satire. A dedicated online community of Dogecoin enthusiasts nonetheless emerged spontaneously as people began exchanging the coin between them along with memes of the Japanese Shibe-Inu dog that Markus and Palmer chose as the coin symbol. It was not long before specialized Dogecoin channels and forums were established on Twitter, Reddit, Facebook and Telegram. Conversations between supporters contributed to the tides of high and low characterizing the dynamic of selling and buying in cryptocurrency exchange platforms at large. The online community of users, in short, with their feel-good discourse and quirky humour, has steadily raised the financial value of Dogecoin as a byproduct of their ongoing interactions. Together, community members invented almost by accident new online spaces for communitarian debates, which are still bustling with economic activity to this day.

Other such 'communities' even purported to set up extrastatist political entities online (Faria 2019). The now debunked 'BitNation', for example, used a blockchain that enabled individuals to create 'borderless' communities using a decentralized coin mischievously called 'Xpat' (Atzori 2017: 48). Although the project failed ideologically and economically (Faria 2022), in the years in which it existed online, BitNation actively encouraged people all over the world to engage in political structures of their own creation. The blockchain can be seen in both these cases as 'cosmogram' (Brunton 2019), a pragmatic utility item that both symbolizes a theory of the social universe (i.e. its aspired decentralized structure) and inspires the structuration of a shared sociality among supporters. The act of exchange itself becomes the mundane realization of myths that organize the origin and boundaries of the community while also representing individual members as romantic heroes at the brink of a social and economic revolution (Faustino et al. 2022). From my own experience, this gnostic dimension accompanies most new crypto projects, even those that aim towards financial pragmatism, at least at the discursive level.

In a landmark study, Lana Swartz (2017) demonstrated that blockchain gnostic theories are in fact ideologically diverse. Swartz (ibid) distinguishes analytically between 'incorporative blockchain dreamers', who seek the integration of blockchain into existing 'centralized' systems, on the one hand, and 'radical blockchain dreamers', who propagate the invention and use of new 'decentralized' technological solutions that will eventually bring to the collapse of the established socioeconomic system, on the other hand (Faustino et al. 2022). Swartz argues that while 'incorporative' efforts are conformist in nature – i.e. they do not break with hegemonic morality – 'radical' blockchain discourse generates a *cultural critique* at the forefront of digital capitalism (Dodd 2018: 36; Greenfield 2018). Swartz focuses on the inherent tension existing between these two approaches, which propose distinct technomoral frameworks, the first promoting a quasi-utopian transformation of capitalism from within and the second engaging in quasi-millenarian and often iconoclastic ventures to revise deeply embedded cultural norms in the West concerning trust, ownership and power (Faria 2019; Shapiro 2022).

Contrary to Foucault's notion of 'governmentality' – which he saw as a force pulling citizens towards docility and compliance with government logic (Foucault 2004) – blockchain-based social governance empowers users to curtail their dependence on state structures at least symbolically. When applied in the context of a 'decentralized' social organization, blockchain-based governance turns this form of radical individualism into the epicentre of new collective identities. This apparent paradox – searching for spiritual or intellectual unity (which blockchain advocates call 'consensus') through structural fragmentation – crystallizes previous forms of libertarian digital mobilization (e.g. May 1992; Barlow 1996) into isolated cultural, political and economic forms of techno-economic activism.

But how do these dynamics of communal-economic encapsulation coincide with the wider global context, in which cryptocurrencies are mere units of exchange or storage of value used at a huge scale? How can, as Nigel Dodd (2018) asked, this money technology be simultaneously ideological and pragmatic? And if it is a vector of identity and a unifying collective symbol, how can it simultaneously attract the hundreds of millions of oblivious potential users who do not necessarily support ideological revisionism? Some insights from sociological crowd theory may provide preliminary answers to these questions.

Crowd Morphology

Elias Canetti (1984 [1960]) famously claimed that the formation of crowds is a truly self-regulating (or self-referential) dynamic phenomenon, wherein smaller groups within the wider mass – and the numerous individuals from which this mass is made – might always separate again as they associate with others and then regroup. Canetti describes this dynamic as a tension between 'closed' and 'open' crowds, the latter being crowds that keep growing as they continuously attract new recruits, and the former being groups that 'renounce growth and put the stress on permanence' (ibid.: 17). Canetti uses this distinction to explain how the apparent fluidity and disorganization of 'open' crowds may lead to stagnation, stability and the concentration of power in 'closed' crowds, which may nonetheless begin to fragment and become open again, in a circular fashion.

This dynamism includes a sense of danger, chaos and havoc precisely because it is perceived as self-brewing and hard to control. From the beginning of the twentieth century until at least the 1970s, different writers, thinkers, journalists and politicians deemed the morphology of crowds anarchic, to the extent that crowds have become a societal risk, a force to be supressed and controlled (Tarde 2007; cf. Beck and Kewell 2014: 111–28). Beck and Kewell write that 'by the 1920s there was a consensus . . . that crowds, mobs, and other forms of spontaneous political gatherings and movement [*sic*] represented one of the principal threats to modern society, its stability and sustainability' (2014: 127). The image of mass media as inherently sensationalist and corrupting, accompanied by the view of modern mass society as a pretext to totalitarianism (cf. McClelland 1989; Borch 2012: 170), further crystallized the idea that crowds are emotional bombshells lacking intellectual integrity or reason (Brighenti 2010 and 2014), a violent and unpredictable phenomenon instigated by warmongers and charismatic leaders that promote totalitarian doctrines in the guise of catchy and easily digestible ideas. Popular representations of crowds still adhere to such views. Think, for example, of terms like 'crowd control' and the irrationality admitted to grand scale mobility based on the consumption of 'fake news' (Lee 2017; Hayden 2021).

Some of the criticism directed towards cryptocurrencies also assumes this negative stance. Critics often cast supporters as a dangerous and disorganized crowd, a random aggregation of people lacking direction or morality. Ideas about crypto as a tax evasion scheme, on the one hand, or a 'financial sect', on the other hand, both of which are prevalent online, designate coin-community members as a criminal mob in the first instance and as a dogmatic flock of worshipers in the second. In both cases critiques focus on the high volatility of the crypto market and its uncontrolled value fluctuations, which opponents attribute to the contagious waves of selling and buying that occasionally involve millions of investors across the globe and result in hectic gains or devastating losses for those who are not fast or alert enough. From a sceptical perspective, it is not libertarian ideology itself that inhibits mass adoption as it is the irrationality and violence of its crowd ontology, exemplified in the chaos of such 'waves'.

A parallel scholarly tradition has however been scrutinizing the negative image of crowds in the last few decades (Baudrillard 1985; Borch 2012; Brighenti 2014; Mazzarella 2017). This scholarly literary corpus considers the energy we feel in our bodies when we take part in a gathering as a form of collective effervescence (Durkheim 1995 [1912]), which brings people into emotional (or even physical) immersion. Elias Canetti claimed that for that reason, *crowds are a universe of egalitarian affect*, a space and time in which everybody is equal and nobody is in command, an experience that temporarily overcomes people's instinctive fears from being touched 'by the unknown' (1984: 15). In this view, the unity between individuals and the mass *liberates* people from both real and imagined inhibitions. Christian Borch (2009: 285) summarizes this well:

> It is only by uniting closely with others that the individual acquires the rare opportunity to emancipate himself or herself from the burdens that have accumulated in him or her and hence to understand himself or herself in new ways . . . [this] even amounts to a democratic transformation: the crowd incident destabilizes existing power structures, creates a momentary equality and freedom, and in that sense empowers the individual in a common act. As a part of this, power and politics are no longer imposed on the individual from outside but emerge from within in a joint enterprise of total equality.

Elaborating this stance, Borch and Knudsen (2013) argue that the morphology of crowds have in fact in recent years become an indispensable aspect of personalized conduct, a literal motivating force that mobilizes people. This conclusion is intuitive when we think of consumer behaviour, but it also offers an exciting framework to analyse the emergent construction of other socioeconomic and political realities. The events of the 'Arab Spring', the flocking of people to join ISIS and the storming of Capitol Hill in Washington DC are all examples for mass mobilization that had no apparent centralized organization apart from a strong common belief in certain values. In all these cases, the emergence of a critical mass of people also included a 'deep' personal transformation, after which individuals felt *compelled* to act. They thus initially conglomerated together as ad hoc crowds, but quickly formed communalist links between them. Borch and Knudsen (2013: 111) identify three main domains in which crowds are re-emerging as significant social forces in the present hyperglobalized world. 'The first', they argue:

> is the political domain, with protesting and occupying crowds (Occupy Wall Street, Los Indignados, etc.) that express explicit political protest. The second manifestation

of postmodern crowds appears within the broad field of sports, leisure, and consumption, where collective energy is focused on high-profile brands, fan communities and event crowds (whether as sports events, festivals, markets, or the like). Finally, a third form of postmodern crowding, which traverses the other two, relates to new digital social media where crowding is produced around certain agendas, issues, and hot topics' (brackets in origin).

I understand the emergent construction of cryptocrowds as a part of this wider phenomenon, wherein people harness the power of multiplicities to produce individual 'freedoms' while simultaneously recruiting the power of individual autonomy to produce new kinds of collective organizations. The mass of 'peer-to-peer' exchange relations in unregulated markets, enabled by the blockchain, can thus be seen to facilitate the emergence of heterogenic postmodern crowds composed of cryptocurrency ideologues, traders, miners, technologists and entrepreneurs. These individuals respond *rationally* to the affective floods that influence all three domains identified by Borch and Knudsen (2013), acting at once as political crowds (in a pragmatic rather than an ideological sense) and as playful crowds hunting for thrills, especially as relating to the FOMO access to legendary fortunes. The authors contributing to this volume considered these cognitive and emotional components as they explored emergent forms of crowds and communities in cryptocurrency and blockchain sociality.

The Book

This volume develops anthropological perspectives on community and crowd dynamics among cryptocurrency adopters across the globe. Each contribution explores either an ethnographic case study or interrogates the philosophy of decentralized markets.

Bruno Campos Cardoso's chapter focuses on the spread of Bitcoin in Brazil. Scrutinizing the heuristic notion of 'hyperbitcoinization' – an accelerated adoption of Bitcoin by many individuals in society, after which Bitcoin will become more dominant than state-produced currencies – Campos Cardoso demonstrates how Bitcoin 'maximalists' (cf. Swartz 2018; Shapiro 2022) in Brazil outline an imagined future of prosperity in a world that proponents believe will soon face a devastating economic collapse. Cardoso argues that the system-specific temporalities of Bitcoin push both for speculative futures organized around the expectation that Bitcoin becomes the main value-mechanism in such postapocalyptic economy and for a resurgence of right-wing radicalization of digital crowds in the Brazilian society at large.

Dimitrios Tsavelis' chapter explores the increasing contemporary 'appification' of money. In this process, money is embedded into digital applications and thus loses its distinctive economic sense, becoming instead a form of communication or media (Swartz 2020). In cryptocurrency sociality, Tsavelis argues, blockchain accelerates this process because it completely differentiates value from politics, turning the exchange of monetary and economic values into a subproduct of any form of communicational interaction (cf. Maurer et al. 2013). The appification of money in crypto thus produces narrative structures that enable masses of cryptocurrency adopters to constitute new types of collective boundaries. Tsavelis claims that despite the global visibility of the blockchain and its alleged wide-ranging implications, these masses paradoxically remain invisible, embedded in the technologies they utilize as mediums of exchange.

Studying crypto-prediction markets, wherein people bet on future events using cryptocurrencies, Anthony J. Pickles' chapter discusses his interlocutors' support in 'futarchy' – a decentralized world *entirely governed* by prediction markets. He argues that futarchy becomes a key factor in gamblers' perception of themselves as rational individuals who nonetheless (and somewhat paradoxically) also consciously appeal to the 'wisdom of crowds' as an organizing social force. He argues that this duality constitutes an impossible tension, whose ironic result is a crowd full of 'cunning' individuals who always seek to work *against the collective thinking of the crowd*, as they try to maximize their individual profits. This fascinating chapter is merely a first step towards further research on the links between prediction, decentralization and the wider anthropological focus on divination and myth in the context of grassroots economies.

Anna Vennonen's chapter uses phenomenological crowd theory (Borch 2007; Stage 2013) to discuss how cryptocurrency adopters in Finland (but also across the globe, as they interact online) experience the forces of the market. Focusing on affect, Vennonen shows that adopters are not necessarily always acting in accordance with the myth of rational individualism, which is still dominant both within the circles of crypto supporters and beyond it, partly due to media coverage that merely focuses on the economic prospects of trading (cf. Buterin 2015a). Rather, she argues, cryptocurrency trading is primarily experiential, a social engagement driven symbolically as much as it is subjected to utilitarian calculations of loss and gain. Vennonen convincingly shows how affect works to both consolidate online cryptocommunities and to set them apart.

Mitch Tuddenham's chapter critically explores the purported horizontality of blockchain interactions. Rather than accepting 'as-is' the idea that blockchain constitutes a structural 'de-hierarchization' of social relations – an idea rooted in the imagination of society as an assembly of fully disengaged yet individually autonomous subjects – Tuddenham argues that the blockchain is in fact a 'transindividuating' machine. By this he means that the blockchain, as a stage for cryptocurrency exchange, initiates processes that go *into* humans as much as they distribute humans across geographical and virtual spaces (cf. Rio and Smedal 2008). Turning away from the vertical-horizontal axis – along with the centre-periphery relationship it implies – Tuddenham argues that cryptocommunities hold the seed of humanity-scale philosophical awakening as much as they are committed to humanity-scale economic (or material) revival.

Finally, the Conclusion builds on my own research in a Bitcoin social club in Tel Aviv. I briefly summarize the contributions of each chapter to a wider application of crowd theory in the realm of cryptocurrency and blockchain sociality. I then suggest that these new insights open up a new way to think of the 'curious' relations between open and closed digital collectives in the world of crypto. I elaborate this analysis theoretically to go beyond structural analyses of the blockchain, widely defined as more or less static descriptions of sociality, focusing instead on the kinds of forces and tensions that may inspire the dynamics of dispersion and enclosure of crypto-communities. I raise the assumption that exchange on the blockchain and interaction in relevant forums are therefore the driving force of a new online sociality, which I attribute to digitalization. I then characterize other contemporary processes that predominantly rely on the movement of masses through cyberspace. The intrinsic connectivity between singularities and multiplicities in the formation of crypto crowds is thus seen as only one aspect of a much wider contemporary phenomenon, which intermittently constitutes 'individuals' (or 'peers'), 'communities' and massive crowds as real or felt entities. These coinciding scales of reference, I conclude, increasingly become crucial to define new forms of association in the lives of cryptocurrency adopters.

Acknowledgements

This publication is based on a workshop that was funded by the ERC Grant Surveillance and Moral Communities (SAMCOM), ID: 947867. Many thanks to Dr Vita Peacock, Principle Investigator (PI) in the SAMCOM research project and grant holder, for having supported this workshop and the consequent publication. I thank the authors who have worked hard to rethink their ethnographic and theoretical material in terms of crowd theory. I am grateful to Roland Kapferer and Don Handelman for their insightful comments and productive debate at the workshop, as well as Christian Borch, whose prolific writing on crowd dynamics inspired me in the first place to think of Bitcoin in crowd theory terms. I send a special thank-you to Photini Vrikki, who ran the KCL series of workshops on digital crowds, and to Bruce Kapferer, Odin of the contemporary academic Asgard, for the ongoing intellectual support and for making this book possible.

Matan Shapiro is a social anthropologist currently researching synoptic surveillance and changing notions of alterity online as part of the European Research Council (ERC)-funded Surveillance and Moral Communities (SAMCOM) Project at the department of Digital Humanities, King's College London.

References

Anderson, Benedict. 2016 [1983]. *Imagined Communities: Reflections on the Origin and Spread of Nationalism*. London: Verso.

Atzori, Marcella. 2017. 'Blockchain Technology and Decentralized Government: Is the State Still Necessary?' *Journal of Governance and Regulation* 6(1): 45–62.

Barbrook, Richard, and Andy Cameron. 1996. 'The Californian Ideology.' *Science as Culture* 6(1): 44–72. Available online: http://dx.doi.org/10.1080/09505439609526455 (accessed 15 June 2023).

Barlow, John Perry. 1996. 'A Declaration of the Independence of Cyberspace.' *Electronic Frontier Foundation*. Available online: https://www.eff.org/cyberspace-independence (accessed 15 June 2023).

Baudrillard, Jean. 1985. 'The Masses: The Implosion of the Social in the Media'. *New Literary History* 16(3): 577–89.

Beck, Matthias, and Beth Kewell. 2014. *Risk: A Study of its Origins, History and Politics*. Singapore: World Scientific Publishing.

BitNation website. Retrieved 15 August 2023 from https://tse.bitnation.co.

Borch, Christian. 2007. 'Crowds and Economic Life: Bringing an Old Figure Back in'. *Economy and Society* 36(4): 549–57. DOI:10.1080/03085140701589448.

———. 2009. 'Body to Body: On the Political Anatomy of Crowds'. *Sociological Theory* 27(3): 271–89.

———. 2012. *The Politics of Crowds: An Alternative History of Sociology*. Cambridge: Cambridge University Press.

Borch, Christian, and Britta Knudsen. 2013. 'Postmodern Crowds: Reinventing Crowd Thinking', *Distinktion: Scandinavian Journal of Social Theory* 14(2): 109–13. DOI:10.1080/1600910X.2013.821012.

Brighenti, Andrea Mubi. 2010. 'Tarde Canetti and Deleuze on Crowds and Packs'. *Journal of Classical Sociology* 10(4): 291–314.

———. 2014. *The Ambiguous Multiplicities: Materials, Episteme and Politics of Cluttered Social Formation*. London: Palgrave Macmillan.

Brunton, Finn. 2019. *Digital Cash: The Unknown History of the Anarchists, Utopians, and Technologists Who Created Cryptocurrency*. Princeton: Princeton University Press.

Buterin, Vitalik. 2015a. 'Superrationality and DAOs'. *Ethereum*. Available at: https://blog.ethereum.org/2015/01/23/superrationality-daos/ accessed in February 2021.

———. 2015b. Visions, Part 2: 'The Problem of Trust'. *Ethereum Blog*. Retrieved 15 August 2023 from https://blog.ethereum.org/2015/04/27/visions-part-2-the-problem-of-trust.

Buterin, Vitalik. 2017. 'The Meaning of Decentralization.' *Medium* 6 February. Available online: https://medium.com/@Vitalik Buterin/the-meaning-of-decentralization-a0c92b76a274 (accessed 15 September 2023).

Canetti, Elias. 1984 [1960]. *Crowds and Power*. New York: Farrar, Straus & Giroux.

Delanty, Gerard. 2003. *Community*. London: Routledge.

Dodd, Nigel. 2018. 'The Social Life of Bitcoin'. *Theory, Culture & Society* 35(3): 35–56.

Durkheim, Emile. 1995 [1912]. *The Elementary Forms of Religious Life*, trans. Karen E. Fields. New York: The Free Press.

Faria, Inês, 2019. 'Trust, Reputation and Ambiguous Freedoms: Financial Institutions and Subversive Libertarians Navigating Blockchain, Markets, and Regulation'. *Journal of Cultural Economy* 12(2): 119–32.

———. 2022. 'When Tales of Money Fail: The Importance of Price, Trust, and Sociality for Cryptocurrency Users'. *Journal of Cultural Economy* 15(1): 81–92 DOI:10.1080/17530350.2021.1974070.

Faustino, Sandra, Inês Faria and Rafael Marques, 2022. 'The Myths and Legends of King Satoshi and the Knights of Blockchain'. *Journal of Cultural Economy*. DOI:10.1080/17530350.2021.192 1830.

Foucault, Michel. 2004. *Security, Territory, Population: Lectures at the Collège de France, 1977–78*, Michel Senellart (ed.), Graham Burchell (trans.). Basingstoke: Palgrave Macmillan.

Golumbia, David. 2016. *The Politics of Bitcoin: Software as Right-Wing Extremism*. Minneapolis: University of Minnesota Press.

Greenfield, Adam. 2018. *Radical Technologies: The Design of Everyday life*. New York: Verso.

Hayden, Cori. 2021. From Connection to Contagion. *Journal of the Royal Anthropological Institute* (N.S.) 27: 95–107.

Hayek, Friedrich A. 1980 [1948]. *Individualism and Economic Order*. Chicago: University of Chicago Press.

Hayes, Adam. 2019. 'The Socio-technological Lives of Bitcoin'. *Theory, Culture & Society*: 1–24.

Lee, L.M. Raymond. 2017. 'Do Online Crowds Really Exist? Proximity, Connectivity and Collectivity'. *Distinktion: Journal of Social Theory* 18(1): 82–94. DOI:10.1080/1600910X.2016.1218903.

Maddox, Alexia, Supriya Singh, Heather Horst and Greg Adamson. 2016. 'An Ethnography of Bitcoin: Towards a Future Research Agenda'. *Australian Journal of Telecommunications and the Digital Economy* 4(1): 65–78. Retrieved 15 August 2023 from https://pdfs.semanticscholar.org/f849/538ff2fb784e294433b3812d19719a3bc017.pdf.

Maurer, Bill. 2016. 'Re-Risking in Realtime on Possible Futures for Finance after the Blockchain.' *Behemoth: A Journal on Civilization* 9(2): 82–96.

Maurer, Bill, Taylor Nelms and Lana Swartz. 2013. '"When Perhaps the Real Problem Is Money Itself!": The Practical Materiality of Bitcoin'. *Social Semiotics* 23(2): 261–77.

May, Timothy. 1992. 'Libertaria in Cyberspace.' *Satoshi Nakamoto Institute*. Available online: https://nakamotoinstitute.org/libertariain-cyberspace/ (accessed 15 September 2023).

Mazzarella, William. 2017. *The Mana of Mass Society*. Chicago: University of Chicago Press.

McClelland, John. 1989. *The Crowd and the Mob: From Plato to Canetti*. London: Unwin Hyman.

Nakamoto, Satoshi. 2008. 'Bitcoin: A Peer-to-Peer Electronic Cash System'. *Open Access Online*. Available online: https://bitcoin.org/en/bitcoin-paper (accessed 15 September 2023).

Nelms, C. Taylor, Bill Maurer, Lana Swartz and Scot Mainwaring. 2018. 'Social Payments: Innovation, Trust, Bitcoin, and the Sharing Economy'. *Theory, Culture and Society* 35(3): 13–33.

Popper, Nathanial. 2015. *Digital Gold: The Untold Story of Bitcoin*. Harmondsworth: Penguin.

Rio, Kunt, and Olaf Smedal. 2008. 'Totalization and Detotalization: Alternatives to Hierarchy and Individualism'. *Anthropological Theory* 8(3): 233–54.

Scott. Brett. 2014. 'Vision of a Techno-Leviathan: The Politics of the Bitcoin Blockchain'. *Current Anthropology* 37(3): 395–428.

Shapiro, Matan. 2022. 'Crypto-egalitarian Life: Ideational and Materialist Approaches to Bitcoin'. *Social Analysis: The International Journal of Anthropology* 66(3): 62–82. DOI:10.3167/sa.2022.660304.

Simmel Georg. 2005. *The Philosophy of Money*. London: Routledge

Stage, Carsten. 2013. 'The online crowd: A contradiction in terms? On the potentials of Gustave Le Bon's crowd psychology in an analysis of affective blogging.' *Distinktion: Scandinavian Journal of Social Theory* 14(2): 211–26. DOI: 10.1080/1600910X.2013.773261.

Swartz, Lana. 2017. 'Blockchain Dreams: Imagining Technoeconomic Alternatives after Bitcoin', in Manuel Castells (ed.), *Another Economy Is Possible: Culture and Economy in a Time of Crisis*. Cambridge: Polity, pp. 82–105.

———. 2018. 'What Was Bitcoin, What Will It Be? The Technoeconomic Imaginaries of a New Money Technology'. *Cultural Studies* 32(4): 623–50.

———. 2020. *New Money: How Payment Became Social Media*. New Haven: Yale University Press.

Tarde, Gabriel. 1903. *The Laws of Imitation*, trans. Else Clews Parsons. *New York: Henry Holt and Company.*

———. 2007. 'Economic Psychology', trans. Alberto Toscano. *Economy and Society* 36(4): 614–43. DOI:10.1080/03085140701615185.

Turner, Fred. 2006. *From Counterculture to Cyberculture: Stewart Brand, the Whole Earth Network, and the Rise of Digital Utopianism*. Chicago: University of Chicago Press.

Zimmer, Zac. 2017. 'Bitcoin and Potosí Silver: Historical Perspectives on Cryptocurrency'. *Technology and Culture* 58(2): 307–34.

Zuboff, Shoshana. 2019 *The Age of Surveillance Capitalism: The Fight for a Human Future at the New Frontier of Power*. New York: Public Affairs.

TOWARDS HYPERBITCOINIZATION
Bitcoin Maximalism as Speculative Fiction

Bruno Campos Cardoso

Introduction

Brazil has seen a significant increase in the adoption of cryptocurrencies in recent years, with a growing number of individuals and businesses using Bitcoin and other cryptocurrencies for transactions and investments. During the second wave of the COVID-19 pandemic in the beginning of 2021, with hundreds to thousands of deaths per day, the Brazilian Stock Exchange was also hitting records in its transaction volumes. The Bovespa Index reached its all-time-high (ATH) in early January that year. Bitcoin was rising in value every week from November 2020 onwards, hitting its ATH price a few months later, when one Bitcoin (BTC) was being traded for up to US$60,000 (around 300,000 Brazilian reals (BRL) at the time). Since 2018, the number of individual investors in cryptocurrencies in Brazil was already twice the number of individual investors in the traditional financial market, with both numbers growing steadily to this day.[1]

The disjointed nature of the Brazilian sociopolitical catastrophe and the apparent exuberance of the crypto and stock markets are some of the most striking aspects of the neoliberal economics and austerity politics – as David Graeber puts it, it's in fact more of 'a political project dressed up as an economic one' (Graeber 2018: xxii) – enforced by former President Jair Bolsonaro's government and backed by Brazilian elites. These very different realities diverge further apart when we start asking what kind of social futures are being imagined by different groups of economic actors, from the stock markets but especially from the crowds at the verge of cryptocurrency market systems.

In this chapter I focus on Brazilian digital communities of so-called *Bitcoin Maximalists*, a growing cult-like global movement of orthodox Bitcoin-only users, whose future-fictions imagine 'citadels' populated by sovereign individuals and powered by transactions settled on the Bitcoin blockchain, a utopian society that would be born throughout a speculative and unstoppable process they often refer to as *hyperbitcoinization*. This hypothetical, albeit highly anticipated, phenomenon is most famously defined by an early prominent Bitcoiner Daniel Krawisz as 'a voluntary transition from an inferior currency to a superior one, and its adoption is a series of individual acts of entrepreneurship rather than a single monopolist that games the system' (Krawisz 2014). For Bitcoin *Maxis*, deep 'in the rabbit hole' of allegedly Bitcoin financial disruption, this is a most desirable outcome for the electronic peer-to-peer cash development and large-scale adoption.

This hypercapitalist framing of the future resembles Mark Fisher's definition of *capitalist realism*, 'the widespread sense that not only is capitalism the only viable political and economic system, but also that it is now impossible even to imagine a coherent alternative to it' (Fisher 2009). As *capitalist realism* is, on the one hand, a material constraint on the collective political imaginations of Western societies, *hyperbitcoinization* is, on the other hand, a deliberately crowding endeavour towards a *hypercapitalist realism* where all political and economic imaginations are sucked into Bitcoin's black hole. Following Fisher on his Foreword for the book *Economic Science Fictions* (Davies 2018), it might seem quite paradoxical that capital constrains alternative imaginations as such, and yet, as he argues, 'far from being a system liberated *from* fictions, capitalism should be seen as the system that liberates fictions to rule over the social' (ibid.: xii). Moreover, Fisher asks 'what is capital "itself", if not an enormous effective virtuality, an inexorably expanding black hole that grows sucking social, physical and libidinal energies into itself?' (ibid.: xiii). Paraphrasing Fisher's well-known definition, what I mean by hyperbitcoinization is the extremist belief that not only Bitcoin is the only viable political and economic system, but also, according to its most vocal crowd of advocates, that it should be impossible even to imagine a better alternative to it.

Bitcoin maximalism articulates the idea that there can be only one true decentralized cryptocurrency, which happens to be Bitcoin, the first and currently most widespread one. Bitcoin maximalism is also based on the belief that Bitcoin as a decentralized system, as a set of algorithms and *mining* machines, provides a superior kind of money and a better set of monetary rules than any other cryptocurrency or nation-state currencies. This term gained general relevance in cryptocurrency digital communities after a 2014 blog post by Ethereum founder Vitalik Buterin, in which he criticized the 'dominant maximalism' of Bitcoin, referring to this Maximalist perspective as 'the idea that an environment of multiple competing cryptocurrencies is undesirable, that it is wrong to launch 'yet another coin,' and that it is both righteous and inevitable that the Bitcoin currency comes to take a monopoly position in the cryptocurrency scene'.[2]

Buterin's critique was later appropriated and adopted by *maxis* themselves as a virtuous and morally superior position regarding the cryptocurrency ecosystem. For instance, on social networks like Twitter, you might spot this rather radical crowd by their profile pictures with photoshopped red-laser eyes; their endless and sometimes mindless replication of slogans and *memes* about Bitcoin superiority; conservative Christian-inspired moral and behavioural statements; the alleged benefits of red-meat-only diets; and the glorification of neoclassical economics and capitalism itself. The publication of *The Bitcoin Standard* by Saifedean Ammous in 2018 (which was later translated into Brazilian Portuguese in 2020) is one of the many publications that further established and popularized this perspective as a cultural movement among the digital crowds of cryptocurrency enthusiasts.

In Brazil, this movement is mainly articulated throughout social networks such as Twitter, YouTube and Instagram, frequently blending itself among the far-right and neoliberal digital communities as a rather unstructured set of imperatives for collective market-oriented decision making, powered by the desire to gain control over their own financial futures through self-custody of cryptoassets and financial autonomy. In the following sections I argue that the concept of hyperbitcoinization works as a crowding framework informed by what is often called 'cryptoeconomics' and cyberlibertarian ideologies in the formation of group identities, in such a way that the idea of hyperbitcoinization is one of the 'core beliefs' among Bitcoin Maximalists in Brazil and worldwide, a movement which closely tied with the far-right-wing radicalization of digital communities alike.

Self-Fulfilling Hypes

'Bitcoin is an innovation on the order of agriculture, antibiotics, or the industrial revolution' says one Bitcoin *maxi* on Twitter,[3] encapsulating in a brief statement some of the tropes of hyperbitcoinization as a revolutionary process already under way.

In a series of online exchanges with Brazilian Bitcoiners during the pandemic, I was told by a *maxi* that the expected disruption of economy might be due to occur much earlier than expected. According to him, a self-described entrepreneur and investor in his late twenties, 'the hyperbitcoinization of society' will inevitably occur since Bitcoin is a scarce asset in the face of the current aggressive expansion of nation-state monetary bases around the globe, citing as an example the exponential rise of gold prices against the German mark in the 1920s and 1930s. 'Gradually, then suddenly', so the slogan goes. Implicit in this comparison is the idea that monetary inflation through 'money printing' leads to hyperinflationary processes where scarce assets, such as gold or Bitcoin, will rapidly appreciate in value because of their intrinsic properties, making them a superior form of money ('hard money' or 'sound money') against nation-state fiat currencies, which are doomed to fail 'by default'.

This perspective on fiat currencies and the traditional financial system was in fact famously articulated by Satoshi Nakamoto himself, the pseudonymous programmer or collective behind the creation of the Bitcoin protocol, in a 2009 forum post announcing the first version release of the Bitcoin client:

> The root problem with conventional currency is all the trust that's required to make it work. The central bank must be trusted not to debase the currency, but the history of fiat currencies is full of breaches of that trust. Banks must be trusted to hold our money and transfer it electronically, but they lend it out in waves of credit bubbles with barely a fraction in reserve. We have to trust them with

our privacy, trust them not to let identity thieves drain our accounts.[4]

Since then, the issue of trust in third-party entities such as banks, along with the imminent risk of currency debasement, is one of the main tropes addressed by cryptocurrency enthusiasts, and arguably the main reason that led to the inception of Bitcoin protocol itself. Because of its programmed scarcity through a tight monetary emission schedule, Bitcoin is viewed by its most ardent advocates as a hedge against the foreseeable economic collapse. The predicted hyperinflationary crisis throughout the world is perceived as a major positive feedback loop that would drive the subsequent waves of Bitcoin price surges, also fuelled by the *fear of missing out* (FOMO) on the Bitcoin bandwagon.

The system-specific temporalities of Bitcoin thus push for speculative futures where Bitcoin becomes the main vehicle for communicating value, which is a particular kind of cybernetic approach to this crowd phenomena of self-fulfilling prophecies. To quote Satoshi Nakamoto once again, in an email message back in the early days of Bitcoin, self-fulfilling prophecies are characterized as a kind of crowd phenomena:

> It might make sense just to get some in case it catches on. If enough people think the same way, that becomes a self-fulfilling prophecy. Once it gets bootstrapped, there are so many applications if you could effortlessly pay a few cents to a website as easily as dropping coins in a vending machine.[5]

Nakamoto's reasoning about Bitcoin's future resonates with sociologist Christian Borch's comments, where he argues that financial markets are characterized by a 'crowd syndrome', a complex interplay of rationality and affect, and of desire and passion (Borch 2007 : 550). Even more closely related, Borch brings up the work of Patricia Adler and Peter Adler on the strategies formulated and pursued by economic actors, based on crowd semantics that affect the realities of the markets: 'if enough people adopt a certain belief (no matter how financially baseless it may be), its ramifications will soon become realized in the market' (Adler and Adler 1984: 103 quoted in Borch 2007: 556).[6]

Just like the Bitcoin emission schedule, which is an eleven-line code function that dictates both how many coins are created per block and the upper limit of coins that will ever be created, this and other internal algorithmic temporalities serve the purpose of creating Bitcoin's digital scarcity and influencing its future market behaviour through a set of specific crowd trading strategies.

Also, according to the Maximalists' point of view, everything that happens in the economy and in the world is somehow always 'good for Bitcoin' in the long term. Even the current crypto market crashes, the meltdown of crypto Ponzi schemes and some insolvent crypto exchanges platforms are all framed as events that tend to 'purify' and pave the path to Bitcoin supremacy. As another Brazilian Bitcoiner once explained to me, the Maximalist's role is essential 'to the Bitcoin ecosystem itself', because it is their own orthodoxy that imposes the limits on what modifications should be allowed in the protocol, as much as their setting of guidelines and best practices on the self-custody of Bitcoins (for example, avoiding third-party services and cryptocurrency exchange platforms) are essential to ensure Bitcoin's monetary dominance in the long term.

Most of the Bitcoiners I have talked to and those whose discussions I follow on online communities do not always use the concept of hyperbitcoinization per se to refer to their realities or to make sense of these alleged processes.

More often than not, they gather around related fictions, myths and dogmas-as-slogans as much as they do around the current Bitcoin price action, as a framework to make sense of the global economy and of their own realities and personal choices. Although the belief of the unavoidable hyperbitcoinization of the global economy might be a common factor among Bitcoin Maximalists, in Brazil and in some of the Brazilian communities I follow more closely, I would like to highlight two particular aspects, which might be applicable to other communities elsewhere.

The first aspect is the broad rejection of any kind of state regulation, in the sense that this is one of the main things that crypto enthusiasts and *maxis*, as a crowd, are actively opposed to. As the regulation of cryptocurrencies and cryptoassets is still in its early stages in Brazil, the two main regulatory agencies – the Securities and Exchange Commission (CVM) and the Central Bank of Brazil (BACEN) – have refrained from stating a clear and definitive position on the matter. There are ambiguities over the proper definition of cryptoassets, over which of the current laws and regulations should apply, and over which regulatory agency should enforce them. Overall, it falls upon users to assume the risks of operating with these new financial instruments, to deal with eventual capital loss, to avoid 'suspicious' financial schemes and to observe the general legislative guidelines on financial transactions within the national territory. Although these boundaries are not always clear or enforced, they generally fall over third-party formations and companies, such as cryptocurrency intermediaries and exchanges, since the very systems along which they operate, due to their distributed nature, cannot be bounded or ruled as traditional markets can or would (Cardoso and Morawska Vianna 2019).

However, it is worth noting that in mid-2019, the Federal Revenue of Brazil (RFB) issued a normative instruction that obliges digital exchanges that operate in Brazil to report every financial transaction occurring within their platforms on a monthly basis. This decision has had a significant impact on Brazilian cryptomarkets, as well as among more radical crypto users, whose fears over increased KYC (Know Your Customer) obligations and government taxation have directed them towards more a vocal opposition against any kind of state intervention on digital markets. Bitcoiners' opposition to regulation often comes with a push forward in the direction of these future fictions, where Bitcoin will take over the world by transcending nation-state financial boundaries, which are perceived as obstacles to the idealized 'free-flowing' digital transactions and trading strategies.

The second aspect is that, since all *fiat currencies* are often understood to be 'doomed' by default, with the BRL being no exception; and since all other cryptocurrencies are about to sink to zero as well (because they are seen as nothing more than fancy and elaborated Ponzi schemes), there is a sense of rush and hurry, which is encapsulated in the somewhat famous slogan of 'stack *sats* and stay humble' (*sats* being Satoshis, the smallest tradable unit of Bitcoin, 1/100,000,000 of a Bitcoin), describing an ongoing process of gradual and disciplined *stacking* of Bitcoins. The slow but steady accumulation of *sats* is depicted as a mandatory self-discipline for all dedicated Bitcoiners, who portray this financial practice as both an exercise of individual sovereignty (a common topic among crypto-influencers) and a way of buying themselves 'a way out' when the BRL, and ultimately the dollar, finally turns into dust. Although the slogan says to 'stay humble' during the stack phase, Bitcoiners also hope of being part of an early financial elite in the making: while in the present a modest stack of *sats* might not be converted into a significant wealth, these savings might make them the future super-rich in a post-hyperbitcoinized world. As a prominent Bitcoin developer summarizes in a tweet:

> Q: What's your bitcoin trading strategy?
> A: Collect as much as possible before the rest of the world catches on.
> That's it, that's the trade.[7]

This particular emphasis on accumulation instead of trading, fuelled by the FOMO on the hyperbitcoinization boom, highlights one of the main characteristics of the *maxi's syndrome*: if, possibly in the near future, all other goods and commodities are going to be denominated and traded for *Bitcoins* and *sats*, there is no point in trading it now for everything else. The crowd-enforced positive feedback loops of accumulation, despite sudden price crashes or long bearish markets, are the main affect that drives *maxis* towards their promised Bitcoin-powered utopias.

The constant production of future fictions somewhat drives these digital communities of Bitcoin enthusiasts towards imagined futures of 'Bitcoin citadels', private cities or small countries inhabited by sovereign individuals, the zero-inflation tax-free computer-driven gun-packed heavens that they actively dream, meme and hype about. That is where, according to them, Bitcoin inevitably leads: a disruption of the social towards a crowd of sovereign individuals.

Hyperbitcoinization as a Crowding Framework

Drawing upon the notion of hyperstition by Nick Land and the CCRU (Cybernetic Culture Research Unit), the media theorist Simon O'Sullivan defines the concept of *mythotechnesis* as the production of technologically enabled and experimental future-fictions that 'feedback on the real'

(O'Sullivan 2017). In this sense, the mythotechnesis of Bitcoin, where the hyperbitcoinization process is its most prominent algorithmic crowding phenomena, unfolds on online platforms as feedback mechanisms from its own promised futures, fed by cyberlibertarian utopias (Winner 1997) over a network of social platforms that facilitate forms of far-right radicalization (DeCook and Forestal 2022).

In the case of Brazil, it is interesting to reflect on the relation between hyperbitcoinization and far-right radicalization within a crowding framework in order to understand how Bitcoin *maxis* often identify and relate to former President Jair Bolsonaro's most ardent supporters, characterized by their 'swarm behavior' and the employment of digital guerrilla techniques (Cesarino 2020; Cesarino and Nardelli 2021).

During Bolsonaro's presidential campaign in 2018 and also his disastrous four-year government, it was very common to spot batches of forwarded propaganda from his political party and his supporters' groups in various cryptocurrency communities. Despite the general sentiment among crypto users that governments are mostly inherently 'evil', Bolsonaro was accepted as both a 'moral conservative' and an 'economic liberal' (mainly in the figure of his assigned Minister of Economy, Paulo Guedes, a Chicago boy himself), thus aligning, albeit loosely, with values shared by some cryptocommunities as an 'outsider' figure that could take national institutions 'out of the way' of sovereign individuals, one small step closer towards their anarchocapitalist dreamland.

In a sense, part of the Brazilian far-right movement has found in cryptocommunities a useful organizational framework for the dissemination of its own right-wing propaganda, given the way in which neoliberal ideologies are facilitated and deeply encoded in cryptocurrency systems.

Both the far-right and crypto enthusiasts present themselves as anti-system, gathering to deploy an anti-establishment political and economic alternative, overemphasizing the rhetoric of 'free markets' and 'individual freedom' of trade and of enterprise.

Although there is no uniform right-wing movement, let alone a Bitcoin *maxi* one, both converge into the same ecosystem. As David Golumbia (2016) argues: 'Bitcoin activates or executes right-wing extremism, putting into practice what had until recently been theory.' This is to say that Bitcoiners depend on right-wing assumptions about economy and society, as much as they help spreading them throughout their ecosystem and beyond. Instead of conflating both movements, even though they might instantiate one another, their differences may give raise to other material, political and ideological formations; still, according to Golumbia, it is hard to see how one can resist 'the political values that are very literally coded into the software itself' (ibid.).

Either way, the spectral multitudes of pseudonymous traders gather every day in the ecosystem, identifying crowding tendencies in price action charts and betting for or against them, as *maxis* try to maximize their Bitcoin stack. While particular participants mostly see themselves as 'sovereign', making rational decisions and capital allocations, they are always positioning themselves *along* the market crowd of (pseudo)anonymous traders abstracted as price charts and order books: to draw lines, arrows and channels over a series of price candles is to try to predict the flow of the crowd as *price* – or, as Borch puts it, the price as the 'crowd leader', 'the emotional pull of the market' (Borch 2007: 564). To bet against the crowd is to take risks – but to bet *with* the crowd might be even riskier: of being liquidated, short squeezed, capitulated by the sudden runaway drifts of the markets. The hyperbitcoinized crowd sees itself in price charts while enacting in the present the allegedly optimal economic models from the future. It is through the market that they reinforce their political views and see themselves as a powerful crowd.

As many Bitcoin *maxis* are also *node runners*, which means that they run their own private relaying or mining nodes, they also contribute machine power to the Bitcoin decentralized network. *Maxis* are not able to (or, in fact, they seem to strive not being able to) imagine other economic relations beyond the rules of the Bitcoin protocol and/or the imprecise set of moral primitives derived from a new-age neoliberal Christian-inspired individualism. In a sense, their crowd semantics is somewhat equivalent to the behaviour of their running Bitcoin software: they validate transactions and relay communications that are perceived as aligned with the rules of the Bitcoin protocol and their own social consensus, as they also reject and ignore everything else as *noise*. According to Elias Canetti, 'the urge to grow is the first and supreme attribute of the crowd: it wants to seize everyone within reach' (Canetti 1981: 16). And yet, their crowd growth is often cultivated against 'the masses', despite those who are still stuck or might be forever entrapped by the system, and over whom, in the future, they might rule as a more powerful and wealth like-minded crowd of 'remnants':

> Bitcoin is for the Remnant. Crypto is for the masses. The masses are generally on the wrong side of history because of the madness inherent in crowds. They only find themselves 'right' when it's the default position. After the truth, forged forth by the Remnant, finally prevails . . . By the time they're all finally using Bitcoin in the same way they breathe oxygen, the Remnant will be building cities and citadels, terraforming new lands, unlocking intergalactic energy and

inventing cosmic teleportation. The Remnant are the 20% that make possible the 80% in the Pareto distribution.[8]

Conclusion

In this chapter I have attempted to highlight the hypothetical hyperbitcoinization process as a crowding framework through which Bitcoin Maximalists engage and develop their collective utopias and social speculative fictions. In a sense, this functional myth derive from the system-specific temporalities and algorithmic materialities of Bitcoin, informed by specific political, economic and ideological agendas, such as the cyberlibertarian and the right-wing movements.

In Brazil, many of these ideas have been translated and merged into local right-wing radicalization, namely the ardent *bolsonarista* crowd (commonly referred to as 'herd' by their critics, although most Bitcoiners use the same word to refer to *everyone* but themselves): as they might profit from each other's movements in the present because of a shared past and common points of view, the bolsonarista 'patriotic' hysteria might not fit well into these imagined anarchocapitalist landscapes. As allies of occasion who see themselves as outsiders 'oppressed by the system', some far-right groups have embraced cryptocurrencies as means to promote their vision of a decentralized, libertarian society, while cryptocurrency communities have afforded these groups with new opportunities for communication and organization.

By providing a framework for the disruption of current social and economic settings, crypto crowds and the concept of hyperbitcoinization are often challenging existing power structures within global finance and creating new possibilities for social and economic organization. While this disruption creates new opportunities for social and economic organization, the Maximalist utopias and imagined futures that are being weaved in the present are not simply idle fantasies disguised as self-fulfilling prophecies, but future fictions that have the potential to create new realities and reshape the global financial system in the most unexpected ways. Just as these algorithmic informed future fictions might break through as economic black holes, and far-right-wing movements keep developing new strategies to proliferate among digital crowds, hyperbitcoinization might be somehow already haunting us from the future.

Acknowledgements

This study was financed in part by the Coordenação de Aperfeiçoamento de Pessoal de Nível Superior – Brasil (CAPES) – Finance Code 001.

Bruno Campos Cardoso is a Ph.D. candidate in Social Anthropology at the Federal University of São Carlos, Brazil. His current research is about Bitcoin, cryptocurrencies and digital market formations in Brazil.

Notes

1. 'Número de investidores em bitcoin se aproxima do total do Tesouro Direto', *Estadão*, 12 February 2018. Retrieved 23 August 2023 from https://economia.estadao.com.br/noticias/seu-dinheiro,numero-de-investidores-em-bitcoin-se-aproxima-do-total-do-tesouro-direto,70002186901; 'Quantidade de investidores em criptos salta 68% no Brasil, apontam dados da Receita', *InfoMoney*, 8 September 2022. Retrieved 23 August 2023 from https://www.infomoney.com.br/mercados/quantidade-de-investidores-em-criptos-salta-68-no-brasil-apontam-dados-da-receita.
2. Vitalik Buterin, 'On Bitcoin Maximalism, and Currency and

Platform Network Effects', 20 November 2014. Retrieved 23 August 2023 from https://blog.ethereum.org/2014/11/20/bitcoin-maximalism-currency-platform-network-effects.
3. 'Vitalik is 100% right. 'Crypto' ain't gonna do sh*t. But BITCOIN is an innovation on the order of agriculture, antibiotics, or the industrial revolution. I highly recommend buying some of humanity's best money while you can still exchange paper for it.' Retrieved 23 August 2023 from https://t.co/t93sUWb92k.
4. Satoshi Nakamoto, 'Bitcoin Open Source Implementation of P2P Currency', 11 February 2009. Retrieved 23 August 2023 from https://satoshi.nakamotoinstitute.org/posts/p2pfoundation/1.
5. Satoshi Nakamoto email to the Cryptography Mailing List, 16 January 2009. Retrieved 23 August 2023 from https://satoshi.nakamotoinstitute.org/emails/bitcoin-list/23.
6. Adler and Adler 1984 'The market as collective behavior'; Borch 2007: 556.
7. https://twitter.com/lopp/status/1293157604697559046 (retrieved 23 August 2023).
8. Aleksandar Svetski, 'Bitcoiners Are the Remnant', *Bitcoin Magazine*, 21 September, 2021. Retrieved 23 August 2023 from https://bitcoinmagazine.com/culture/bitcoiners-are-the-remnant.

References

Adler, P.A. and P. Adler. 1984. 'The Market as Collective Behavior', in P.A. Adler and P. Adler (eds), *The Social Dynamics of Financial Markets*, Greenwich, CT: Jai Press, pp. 85–105.

Ammous, Saifedean. 2018. *The Bitcoin Standard: The Decentralized Alternative to Central Banking*. Hoboken, NJ: Wiley.

Borch, Christian. 2007. 'Crowds and Economic Life: Bringing an Old Figure Back in'. *Economy and Society* 36(4): 549–73.

Canetti, Elias. 1981. *Crowds and Power*. New York: Continuum.

Cardoso, Bruno Campos, and Morawska Vianna, Catarina. 2019. 'Algorithms and Politics in Brazilian Finance: The Formation of a Cryptocurrencies Market'. Paper presented in the 31st Annual Meeting of the Society for the Advancement of Socio-Economics (SASE), New York, 27–29 June.

Cesarino, Leticia. 2020. 'How Social Media Affords Populist Politics: Remarks on Liminality Based on the Brazilian Case'. *Trabalhos em Linguística Aplicada* 59(1): 404–27.

Cesarino, Letícia and Nardelli, Pedro H. J. 2021. 'The Hidden Hierarchy of Far-Right Digital Guerrilla Warfare'. *Digital War* 2(1-3): 16-20.

Davies, William (ed.). 2018. *Economic Science Fictions*. London: Goldsmiths Press.

DeCook, Julia R., and Jennifer Forestal. 2022. 'Of Humans, Machines, and Extremism: The Role of Platforms in Facilitating Undemocratic Cognition'. *American Behavioral Scientist* 67(5): 629-48.

Fisher, Mark. 2009. *Capitalist Realism: Is There No Alternative?* Winchester: Zero Books.

Golumbia, David. 2016. *The Politics of Bitcoin: Software as Right-Wing Extremism*. Minneapolis: University of Minnesota Press.

Graeber, David. 2018. *Bullshit Jobs: A Theory*. New York: Simon & Schuster, 2018.

Krawisz, Daniel. 2014. 'Hyperbitcoinization', 29 March. Retrieved 23 August 2023 from https://nakamotoinstitute.org/mempool/hyperbitcoinization.

O'Sullivan, Simon. 2017. 'From Financial Fictions to Mythotechnesis', in Henriette Gunkel, Ayesha Hameed and Simon D. O'Sullivan (eds), *Futures and Fictions*. London: Repeater Books, pp. 318-46.

Winner, Langdon. 1997. 'Cyberlibertarian Myths and the Prospects for Community'. *ACM SIGCAS Computers and Society* 27(3): 14-19.

The Sociality of the Blockchain and the Appification of Money
Affordances of a New Paradigm for Crowds

Dimitrios Tsavelis

Introduction

There is currently a significant rise of interest in the 'payment space' from researchers, industry and more recently governing institutions alike – or, as Maurer puts it, 'in that new body forms, adaptations of existing structures, and novel relationships in a variegating ecology of retail payment are coming into being all at once' (Maurer 2017: 215).

Readers with an interest in the payment space are familiar with some of these ways to pay, from cryptocurrency to credit cards, Paypal and, more recently, as payment systems morph into platforms such as WeChat and AliPay (Plantin and De Seta 2019). While not all rely on the bundle of technologies that culminated in the generically known 'smartphone', it is certain that such a significant rise in this practice of digital payments was facilitated by the wider adoption of software and computers.

The digital payment space is characterized by a process of substitution. The mobile phone and the distributed ledger technology displace traditional artefacts as the bank card and cash. This ongoing process is anything but clear. Bratton (2015) tried to theorize this process of computing as global megastructure or, as he calls it, 'The Stack'. Furthermore, money becomes increasingly encoded in computational layers, for instance, through applications and the subsequent practices of digitized transactions.

In this context of computational layering, payment platforms enable the transition of physical crowds into this computational layer, thereby becoming digital crowds. Crowding effects in the crypto space have so far received little attention in terms of conceptualization. This chapter attempts to present a novel conceptualization of crowding effects with regard to the crypto space and distributed ledger technologies. In this space a new notion of value is cast into new configurations of quasi-'invisible crypto crowds'. The chapter will explore the mechanisms of how crowding dynamics on blockchain platforms manifest itself into a new digital crowd paradigm.

Money as Abstraction: The Appification of Money

Money is the primary medium of value transfer in society and is increasingly following the notion of 'economic media' (Beller 2021). As such, it becomes clear that blockchain technologies and their application in the computational and financial domain manifest in an 'embeddedness' of monetary media in the social. In a broader sense, monetary media not only creates information but also manages and assembles it into tradable objects or 'data commodities' (Aaltonen et al. 2021).

Through 'adaptations of existing infrastructures' facilitated via software (see also Maurer 2017), the payment space has expanded beyond simple transactions. Participants in this space are entangled in new practices of scanning, verifying, connecting and interacting – in short, money is becoming 'appified'. The 'appification' of money is visible in the rapid growth of money-related applications across different platforms. Internet banking applications, online payment services such as PayPal, AliPay and WeChat Pay, and platform payment systems such as Apple Pay and Google Pay all encode the payment process in software. In addition, some applications become platform-apps, such as 'digital wallets' (Kenney and Zysman 2016). They will form the connective link to other applications and, as such, will become a central part in the formation of crowds. For instance tickets, reward cards, entrance passes and, more recently, health passes are some of the examples where appification is expanding beyond simple transactions.

With regard to appification, it is easy to see that money and transactions are no longer simply exchanges. The transaction of value becomes a 'mediated interaction' and thus payment configurations become appified. The functionality of money becomes coded in different ways and money moves from a private, local space to a quasi-public global space (Zelizer 2010; Maurer 2017: 48). In this new space the individual essentially becomes part of this computational realm (one could say crowd or community) by executing these novel adaptations of money through streaming, updating, capturing, uploading, linking, saving and scrolling (Chun 2016). Lessig (2006) has argued that computer code configures social relations in comparable ways to law. In what follows, I want to suggest that this new specificity of appification follows the logic of narrativity. In other words, the blockchain can be interpreted as narrative technology.

The Sociality of Distributed Ledger Technologies

The making, structuring and functioning of distributed ledger technologies (blockchains) is best understood through the lens of the concept of 'informating', which is 'the process that translates descriptions and measurements of activities, events and objects into information' (Zuboff 1988: 9). In the age of computation, this implies a reprogramability of our cultural logics and therefore also of crowds. The very existence of blockchain and DLT technology in a wider sense can be critiqued with particular reference to technological solutionism (Morozov 2013) as the technology of distributed ledgers (blockchains) in popular discourse is viewed through a techno-utopian lens of technology with futuristic imaginaries (Dickel and Schrape 2017).

However, it should be noted that with the tokenization of money, distributed ledger technologies essentially remove politics from money. In other words, money is separated from the governing state and banks, and pushed into the wider domain of the 'crowd' and the 'machine'. More broadly, blockchain technology becomes the new digital utopianism of cyberspace. As specified by the elusive Satoshi Nakamoto in a white paper (Nakamoto 2008), the blockchain was developed as the basis for a peer-to-peer electronic cash system, but is now adopted for a variety of application scenarios beyond cryptocurrency and financial transactions (DuPont 2017). The blockchain thus supports the transaction of value through cryptocurrency as an application. As such, distributed ledger technology contributes to the 'appification' of decentralised digital currencies.

The Blockchain as Narrative Technology

The proposed framework to conceptualize blockchain technologies and thereby the byproduct of crypto crowds is 'narrative technologies'. Narrative theory can be used to construct a theoretical framework for understanding technological mediation. Ricoeur believes that if human action can be read and interpreted like written works, then the methods and practices of textual interpretation can function as a paradigm for the interpretation of action for the social sciences. Texts and actions have underlying structures to be explained as well as social meanings to be understood. The core aspect of Ricoeur's works is a narrative theory. Ricoeur's thesis in *Time and Narrative* is that a (hermeneutic) circle exists between human experience and narration: experience has a prenarrative quality that is meaningfully and coherently organized into a story by means of a plot. Time becomes human time to the extent that it is organized in the manner of a narrative; in turn, narrative is meaningful to the extent that it portrays the features of temporal experience (Ricoeur 1980).

The basic feature of a narrative is a plot. The plot picks out, orders and assigns significance to otherwise random and disparate elements by arranging them into an intelligible whole. This structuring activity is what gives the story a meaning and what allows it make its point. Self-understanding is instead mediated by signs, symbols and language, and therefore requires an indirect method of interpretation. A technology on this model is like a text: it is readable, with a meaning that is independent of the intentions of the original creators and users. There is a sizeable class of artifacts that we might call 'identity technologies' – mobile phones, cameras, computers, surveillance equipment and the entire technological network. This implies that the organization of events is made intelligible or, rather, 'followable' (referring to the human ability to 'follow' a story). This makes it possible to interpret the way in which humans 'read' technology (Kaplan 2006: 49). Moreover, Ricoeur (2002: 4) points out that there are certain ways in which humans can construct plots to understand technology – for example, by outlining the motivations for designing a technology.

In other words, I will argue that humans do not read technologies, but that conversely technologies 'read' the human. If we then take Ricoeur's narrative theory seriously, we need to see the 'reading' as a reciprocal process. Therefore, the term 'configuration' is used. In order to defend the claim that technologies configure the narrative understanding, we need to show that – just as with texts – they are involved in the organization of events. I not only want to show that designers use narrative approaches to understand the technologies they create; I also want to go further by showing that technologies themselves configure a plot. According to Ricoeur, we can convincingly support the claim that technologies have the capacity to configure plots, understood as organizations of events. This means that technology closes in on the paradigm of a text. It is therefore also argued that narrative structures mediate all human interactions with technologies.

As a consequence of these methodological assumptions, the narrative capacity of technologies increases whenever technologies get more textual. By analysing technologies according to the way in which they configure a narrative plot or, more specifically, how they organize characters and events in a meaningful whole, it is possible to understand the way in which they inform the social payment space and how this is shaping the notion of value. This framework is concerned with narrative technologies that actively configure our narrative time and instantiate a technological mediation that abstracts from the world of action. Here I will discuss electronic monetary technology as a paradigmatic example:

- Algorithmic trading technologies actively configure narrative time because they 'co-author' the trade narrative.

- Although narrative technologies mediate events (such as trades and transactions), they configure narrative time on a calculative, mathematical level.
- Phenomenologically and hermeneutically speaking, the transaction is about numbers that represent quasi-characters (e.g. blockchain hash function, blocks).

Kaplan argues that narrative theory can be used to interpret the way in which humans 'read' technology (Kaplan 2006: 49). Moreover, he points out that there are certain ways in which humans can construct plots to understand technology – for example, by discussing the motivations for designing a technology (Kaplan 2009: 4). These plots are 'constructed' or, to follow the terminology of Ricoeur, 'configured'. A good example of this configuration process is the emergence of the 'appification' of the payment space through software. Software applications establish a verbal interaction with the system. The system thereby starts to interact with the user. The narrative capacity of technologies increases, whenever technologies get more textual. This is clearly the case with 'software' and 'applications'. Narrative technologies that actively configure our narrative time and instantiate a technological mediation that abstracts from the world of action are the paradigmatic example of this – namely, digital payment systems.

Digital payment systems mediate actual events and actual characters, the narrative they configure, operate on a calculative, mathematical level. In the case of blockchain and digital payment systems, this means a representation of quasi-characters (hash functions and blocks) and quasi-events (payment, exchange and cryptographic order) configured in a quasi-plot (e.g. a blockchain transaction or Apple Pay function). Moreover, the narrative time of electronic monetary technologies is rigorously subjected to chronological time dimensions. Chronological timing of trades is the essence of modern digital payment machines, and the sequence of the operations for the execution of transactions is critical to the functioning of the system.

Consequently, transactions become a matter of calculations, removed from reality, real events and related material realities, or, as Baudrillard has put it: Signs and modes of representation come to constitute 'reality'. A new type of social order in which it is signs and codes that constitute the *real emerges* (Kellner 1989), generated 'by models of a real without origin or reality: *a hyperreal*' (Baudrillard 1994). Blockchain transactions can therefore create data, tokens and a ledger. The ledger preserves all historical transaction information while also producing and circulating the resulting data and tokens. By creating, expressing and recording network activities, transactions enact the ruleset of the blockchain's protocol, determining which data, tokens and histories are configured.

In addition to creating, distributing and recording data transmitted across a network, blockchain transactions involve the creation of currency, the transfer of funds and the circulation of value, with digital tokens functioning as a speculative financial asset and medium of exchange. These digital tokens, in turn, circulate as cryptocurrencies (e.g. Bitcoin) or nonfungible tokens (NFTs) with the capacity to become economic in different ways. Cryptocurrencies and NFTs, for instance, are used as collectibles, financial assets, stores of value, digital money and property. Meanwhile, a diversity of private and permissioned blockchain implementations, often categorized as distributed ledger technologies (DLTs), leverage the functionality of an auditable and distributed log of network events without any tokenizing features to increase and streamline datafication, optimize the production, management, supposed privacy and transparency of big data through encryption, and facilitate the digitized economization of data via extractive measures (Calvão and Archer 2021). The economization of a blockchain transaction vis-à-vis tokenization and the subsequent 'appification' of the payment space warrants further consideration, as it is closely linked to new developing forms of sociality, monetization and crowd theory.

Crowds and Crowding in the 'Narrative' Blockchain

The emergence of digital tokenized payment systems and, in particular, blockchain and its application of cryptocurrencies has similar thematic concepts in common with crowds and crowd theory. Borch and Knudsen (2013) proposed three categories of crowds: the consumer crowd, political crowd and the digital crowd. Within this categorization, digital media acts as a connective thread or as I will call the 'medium' or 'platform' of the crowds. Interestingly, all these three categories of crowds are represented in one way or another within the wider domain of distributed ledger technologies and digital payment systems. First of all, blockchain cryptography was the ideological basis of adopting the application of cryptocurrency and, as such, a political ideological consequence of the cypherpunk ideology. The cypherpunks were 1990s digital activists who challenged government policies aiming to prevent the emergence of unregulated digital cryptography, an online privacy technology capable of escaping government surveillance (Jarvis 2022). Second, digital crowds are the result of the intertwinement of digital media with social life. Digital crowds are enveloped in technospheres of data-rich devices or data-rich environments such as blockchains (Ziada 2020). Third, the consumer crowd has become a growing category of networked publics by the rise of digital media (Boyd 2010) and is characterized by the idea of the 'prosumer' blurring the lines between production and consumption. This leads to the conceptualization of the 'homo economicus' according to Borch (2007) a machine-like rational subject that hints at an interaction between humans and objects as proposed by Latour in Actor-Network-Theory (Latour 2007).

In my view, two concepts in particular can be helpful to further theorize the role of different crowds, crowds play in the domain of blockchain technology/crypto. Deleuze's conceptualization of the machine, including his concept of the social machine (Deleuze 2009). Deleuze rightly suggests that specific forms of human collectivities can be interpreted as machines. Simondon's description of machine space (Simondon et al. 1980), which was also conceptualized as code space by Dodge and Kitchin (2004) where technology actually organizes and configures space for the crowds, thereby leading to the emergence of 'data publics'. Analysing this through the lens of the blockchain domain leads to the realization that within the new machine space of the blockchain, a new manifestation of data publics forms that some also call 'crypto crowds'.

This idea of new data publics or 'crypto crowds' can be further perpetuated and expanded through Baudrillard. Baudrillard posits that the social becomes obsessed with itself through a process called 'auto-information' (Baudrillard and Maclean, 1985), which means we are constantly confronted with the anticipated numerical verification of our behaviour. This heavily automated production of information in the computer age devoid of human involvement works in the background. More recently, this phenomenon was also described as 'datafication' (Lycett 2013) or as O'Dwyer (2019) details the evolution of money's mnemonic function and its historical relationship to record-keeping. From ancient tokens to electronic payment systems, she observes that 'money has always been contiguous and at times indistinguishable from its data' (O'Dwyer 2019: 8).

In a similar fashion, Baudrillard asserts that there is an apparatus of recording/capturing data. In a wider sense this apparatus of recording and capturing is the blockchain's perpetual creation of blocks for each transaction executed on the blockchain. Baudrillard extends his theorization, suggesting that we live in an era of simulation where the masses are simulated and where signs and modes of representation have come to constitute reality – a new type of social order in which it is signs and codes that constitute 'the real' (Kellner 1989: 63) generated 'by models of a real without origin or reality: a hyperreal'.

Indeed, the blockchain imposes a new type of social order where signs and modes of representation (blocks and hash functions) constitute a new reality (verification of a block). These new blocks are generated by the automated system of the blockchain, constituting what Baudrillard describes as new reality: the hyperreal. NFTs in particular are a good example of the formation of a new hyperreal. Castells described a new notion of the real as 'real virtuality'. Baudrillard expands on this: through this apparatus of recording and capturing data, the masses disappear, thereby creating an invisible mass that paradoxically is deeply embedded in the capturing and recording of a cryptographic apparatus of the blockchain, where the mass is invisible, but parts of the data block are open to read for the participating crowds. In other words, exchange value is codified by sign-value; reality fades away in favour of copies or, as Baudrillard asserts, simulation. These copies are represented by the continuous creation of the hash function and the simulation is the 'minting' of new blocks by integrating copies of old information into new realities. Baudrillard describes this process as retransmission of all our facts through a process of automatic writing (Baudrillard 1995). The question here is: *are narrative technologies contributing to this formation of the invisible mass?*

Baudrillard speaks of a world where 'human beings have disappeared' (Baudrillard 2008: 31). However, he is clear that the emphasis is on disappearance, not complete extinction or exhaustion of the subject. According to him, this constitutes a specific form of disappearance (Baudrillard 2008). A possible answer to this question must be that the technology of the blockchain and its various applications or, as Baudrillard terms it, the 'apparatus of recording and capturing' is perpetuating a decoupling process of the individual and the masses and re-arranging the individual through the masses and through the cryptographic process of the blockchain in an invisible fashion.

The Ethnography/Empirical Material

This chapter analyses specific characteristics of the monetization of the social created through a reinterpretation of the notion of value in the blockchain as underlying technology. The object of study is to demonstrate what the affordances of these new forms of digital payment systems are and how the socialization of money is informing the crypto/blockchain start-up space. Combining theoretical blockchain studies and applying the concept of narrative technologies together with ethnographic practices enables a grounded discussion on blockchain-based monetization of the social. The particular ethnographic case example I like to highlight in the context of crowding effects in the blockchain is that of a start-up I interviewed for my research, which allows individuals to take control of their data while monetizing it as a cryptographic asset. This start-up aims to make digital certificates in the form of NFTs using the blockchain. These certificates shall tokenize consumer data as data assets. Effectively, this leads to the creation of social tokens or altered forms of money. In this scenario, we see the formation of data as cultural artefact through the demarcation of the individual and the wider crowd. This resembles what Lana Swartz calls transactional communities (Swartz 2020) and what through the lens of Ricoeur we call narrative identities (Ricoeur 1988).

The founders of this particular application on the blockchain highlighted that for them, monetization begins in the social sphere. Discussing some of the main functions of money – medium of exchange, store of value and unit of account – it soon became clear during this particular interview that the financial part of the blockchain idea is the 'application' or, as one of the founders puts it, 'the NFTs are foundation of the application layer' (Tsavelis 2023). It becomes apparent here that this particular founders are thinking in terms of a layered blockchain space. The abstraction level with regard to the interpretation of money itself goes even further. During the interview, one of the founders mentioned that 'for us digital certificates are the money part of the idea, we are functionalising the concept of money' or, as the co-founder further exemplifies, 'for us money carries content, almost like an NFT' (Tsavelis 2023, Findings section).

From this brief excerpt from the interview, it becomes apparent that the founders of this particular start-up tacitly understand money as content and application. This is indeed very close to the theoretical framework set out by Ricoeur. The idea behind this blockchain start-up is to functionalize money; as such, it cast a new configuration of value through the imposition of certificates (in this case NFTs) as tradeable money alternative. Consequently, by framing money as 'content' or in the wider sense text, two interesting things happen: first, money becomes readable and through tokenization money becomes appified; and, second, in this newly established appified system, the application of money is mediated through narrative structures and therefore different configurations of value become possible. As a result of this configuration process, the social is monetized and this is exemplified by creating a data asset. This textual component framework of Ricoeur now allows us to understand that 'data' is created out of 'data' (see also Zuboff 1988). However, this process is continually perpetuated. The very system of the blockchain and tokenization creates new narrative structures through their now circular configuration in the distributed ledger. This enables not only (as discussed) new notions of value, but also new forms of crypto communities or crypto crowds. At the same time, this process also blurs the lines between what constitutes the public and private appearance of the subject or individual and their eventual mode of disappearance. The result is the formation of a new invisible mass or crowd that also paradoxically is highly visible through the narrative structure of distributed ledger technology and its various applications, especially that of value and money.

Money and Appification: An Anaylsis through Simmel

Software applications in the form of apps have increasingly developed into alternative money systems using a range of media and practices such as peer-to-peer networks to facilitate the exchange of value through 'technological vehicles' such as the blockchain. This is something that Dodd (2012) described as 'perfect money' or 'pure token money' (Simmel 2004: 165). Simmel states that it is token money that is detached from 'every substantial value' (Simmel 2004: 167) and this is also what contributes to social synthesis or, in other words, the formation of crowds. As Simmel puts it, 'every one of its members were fully relationally integrated, each one dependent on all others and all others on the one, just because each one is individually a part of it' (Simmel 2009: 50).

Following Simmel, it is individuals who reproduce crowds through a process of action and interaction. Communities or crowds are becoming 'a set of interactions' (Simmel 2009: 170). Interaction is also a key feature of digital environments from which new communities can be built. As a consequence, the practice of interaction produces information that then acts as a medium of exchange for an individual (Riva and Galimberti 1997). Simmel has argued that money is shifting from the 'material' into more abstract forms towards a state of pure abstraction. In this evolved state of pure abstraction, the formation of crowds is perpetuated. The proliferation of the functional value instead of the intrinsic value of money has led to an expansion of money into the digital space in forms of online payment systems, and pure digital forms of value in the form of cryptocurrency through blockchain technologies. This very expansion into the digital space has enabled a new notion of crowd, namely crypto crowds. Simmel makes two central assumptions about the individual and society, which is of particular relevance to the formation of crowds in the crypto sphere.

Individuals Are Both within and outside Society

Through the process of appification of the money sphere, the tensions between singularities and pluralities are exacerbated. The very process of appification reflects Simmel's elements of the theorization of money. Appification itself is characterized by a process of action and interaction. Within this dyad of action and interaction, 'appification' establishes a regime of calculability where platforms facilitate the formation of new digital crowds vis-à-vis the singularity of the individual user. In the philosophy of money, Simmel (2004) suggests that money is increasingly becoming a 'medium'.

This means that money as a medium works inbetween objects and the individual. Money creates distance and detachment from interaction between individuals. The formation of crypto crowds is therefore categorized into separate calculative spheres. In a similar notion to 'social media', the distinction of private and public versus individual and crowd became blurred. Payment and exchange of value itself became social media and formed through a regime of appified money (Swartz 2020).

In this highly techno-appified space communities materialize and dematerialize into crowds and individual entities. Lustig and Nardi (2015) speak about a complex process of authority and trust in this space. This shapes the formation of crypto crowds. The central idea behind this reasoning is the assumption of the 'rational' individual actor (DuPont 2017) or, in a wider sense, what Golumbia (2009) has termed the cultural logic of computationalism. Golumbia asserts that computationalism perpetuates the idea of 'individualism' and 'singularity'. However, within Golumbia's (ibid.) idea of computationalism, the 'individual' gets integrated into a wider automated system. Consequently, Golumbia talks about essentially two states here. The individual gets displaced as the subject and becomes the object of the crowd. What is important to note here is that the 'computationalist' blockchain turns the individual into an extension of the crypto crowd. This notion is close to more recent ethnographically informed research on cryptocurrency communities (DuPont 2019; Swartz 2020). The sociotechnicality of appification creates data-money communities with individuals who engage under the unified umbrella of the blockchain and some of its central applications (for instance, cryptocurrencies and smart contracts, and NFTs).

Appification creates metastructures that enable routes to interaction as proposed by Simmel's theorization of interaction (2009). These metastructures take the function of infrastructures (Bratton 2015). It is the network that becomes infrastructural to the functioning of the blockchain. In turn, the blockchain becomes infrastructural through providing the architecture for the appification of the payment space. As a consequence, sociotechnicality becomes sociodigitality. It is exactly this sociodigitality that accentuates the embeddedness of monetary media in the social and thus increases the tensions between singularities and pluralities in the techno-appified space. These sociodigital assemblages shape the context in which individuals contribute to the formation of communities through markets in the crypto space (Caliskan 2020). Caliskan makes an important distinction here: private versus public blockchains. An example here is the fintech company Ripple, which is a cryptocurrency controlled by a single entity. Ripple is not a direct competitor to cryptocurrencies per se, but a system for facilitating remittances used by financial institutions. Ripple never expanded beyond this very first group of users. This led to tensions between trader communities and individuals. Traders wanted prices to be volatile in order to achieve higher margins. Platform providers wanted prices to be stable or protect their investments, whereas private cryptocommunity individuals wanted prices to be cheap so they could participate in the community. Thus, individuals drifted towards other blockchain projects (Rella 2020).

Maurer has summarized this as 'blockchain technologies not imposing radically new monetary systems but they rather perform on the level of "plurality" thus highlighting the tensions between embedded and disembedded money practices between communities and individuals' (2012: 415).

Individuals Are Both Objects and Subjects within Networks of Communicative Interaction

In this context, appification explores new modalities of visibility. Objects (blockchains, cryptocurrencies, digital payment platforms and hash functions) and subjects (users and individuals) are structuring and restructuring visibility through a framework of software and coding processes. As analysed at the beginning of this discussion, this new construction of visibility imposes a new notion of invisibility (Baudrillard 1988). These networks of communicative interaction (blockchains and hash functions) form an all-seeing visibility machine with an important feature of 'disappearance' (Foucault 1977). The medium of the 'blockchain' is governing visibility and invisibility at the same time; the medium becomes the message of this new notion of technocrowds (McLuhan 1964). The individual's 'action' is totally seen by other users of the blockchain (Foucault 1977: 202). However, it is not the singular that counts in this arena of the technocrowds, but the plurality and dynamic structure of the blockchain that circulates the formation of crypto crowds through various applications on the blockchain. Cryptocurrencies, wallets and blockchain exchanges are applications of the blockchain that perpetuate these contradictory dynamics. Within this regime, the visibility of the individual becomes the reward for interaction with the invisible 'crypto crowds' of the blockchain. An example of this is the 'miners' of the blockchain who perform 'interaction' work within the blockchain. They inscribe, register and organize mining operations collectively, thereby enabling the formation of pluralities of crypto miners in the crypto space (Calvão 2019; Caliskan 2020).

In this context it is important to point to Simmel's concept of 'sociation'. According to Simmel, 'sociation is the form in which individuals grow together into a unity and within which their interests are realized. And it is on the basis of their interests . . . that individuals form such unities' (Simmel 1971: 24). A good representative example of Simmel's concept of 'sociation' is the practice of splits in the blockchain. Disagreement among communities leads to the formation of new crypto crowds. A particular feature of blockchains is the arrangement and structuring of communities along a chronological chain (Wright and De Filippi 2015). In this sociomaterial dealing with time as the central structuring element, the invisibility of the crowds/groups and the visibility of individuals is not only technologically shaped but also has a social dynamic component (Wajcman 2008).

A useful theoretical construct, to better understand these dynamics of blockchain splits on plurality and singularity, is Actor-Network-Theory (Callon and Latour, 1981). According to Latour (1990), actors can include both social and technical entities (such as individuals, a group of individuals, organizations, ideologies, methodologies and concepts) and artifacts such as hardware and software. This very combination of the social and the technical is what connects Simmel's idea of sociation to how appification and blockchains embed singularities and pluralities through a process of translation where temporality creates alignment within social groups.

Cryptocurrency was one of the first applications of blockchain technology (Nakamoto 2008). The practice of 'splitting' or creating 'forks' of already-existing sociotechnical formations is a prevalent feature of the blockchain. This 'forking' or 'splitting' proposal can be submitted by either individuals or groups. This was also a main theme during the interview with a founder and developer of a so-called application fork in the crypto space. The following quote illustrates how crypto miners can play a central role within the actor-network of appified money:

> miners are like micro-communities, they determine if the blockchain continues . . . (they essentially solve problems for other individuals). This is important, also with regards to the notion of value in the blockchain. Miners remain also a bit opaque . . . they kind of act as background gatekeepers. Somehow miners control the data flows. (Start-up #2: founder and developer) (Tsavelis 2023)

A key finding here is that miners often form groups or pluralities around certain applications as the computing power of an individual is limited in terms of capability. What is even more interesting here is the observation that miners can both be individual actors and also form larger entities (a mining community/pool). This is something that Callon and Latour (1981) described as macro and micro actors:

> the communication of the communities a lot of times is organized on a server on Discord. The exchanges act as kind of more formalized meeting places where individuals and the groups formed on Discord appear and make transactions. (Start-up #2: founder and developer) (Tsavelis 2023)

It is the interaction of community and individuals in the digital payment space that continuously produces a multiplicity of digital crowds that Simmel describes in his concept of 'sociation'. This can range from mundane digital payment assemblages such as digital wallets to more complex systems of blockchains and cryptocurrencies. The movement and circulation of appified money is what sets an analogous function to what Baudrillard (1995, 2008) described as a new mode of disappearance. The visibility of individuals gets augmented, whereas the masses of crypto crowds become invisible.

Summary

By applying the theoretical framework of Simmel's notion of money and analysing the phenomenon of communities/crowds vis-à-vis individuals within the sociotechnical network of digital payment technologies, this chapter has explored the appearance and construction of singularities and pluralities within what Tsavelis (2023) has termed a process of 'appification'. These tensions have been analysed along a two-axis assumption borrowed from Simmel:

1) Individuals are both within and outside society.
2) Individuals are both objects and subjects within networks of communicative interaction.

The presentation and analysis here has developed a new experimental angle on anthropological manifestations regarding the consequences of digital payment systems through the process of appification of the payment space. What this chapter has tried to explore is how individualism and community are paradoxically linked closely together and coexist in the same space, but within different states of visibility or, as Shapiro has put it in the introduction: The 'curious' analytical point is that these dynamics are contradictory' (Shapiro, introduction in this volume) that almost define a new relevance of crowds and crowding phenomena to the emergent construction of new forms of communities.

Acknowledgements

I would like to thank all the individual participants of this Crypto Crowd Workshop for the fruitful discussions and exciting presentations that stimulated a lot of critical thinking around the new and emergent topic of crypto crowds. My thanks go also to my parents and sister for their support during the writing-up stage. Special thanks to Matan Shapiro for his more than notable effort organizing the workshop and making this collected volume possible.

Dimitrios Tsavelis is currently working on his research about dealing with the sociotechnicality and datafication of digital payment systems, with a particular focus on novel, trust less, automated systems of the blockchain.

References

Aaltonen, Aleksi, Cristina Alaimo and Jannis Kallinikos. 2021. 'The Making of Data Commodities: Data Analytics as an Embedded Process'. *Journal of Management Information Systems* 38(2): 401–29. https://doi.org/10.1080/07421222.2021.1912928.

Baudrillard, Jean. 1988. *Simulacra and Simulation. Selected Writings*, Mark Poster (ed.). Stanford: Stanford University Press.

———. 1994. *Simulacra and Simulation*. Ann Arbor: University of Michigan Press.

———. 1995. 'The Virtual Illusion: or the Automatic Writing of the World'. *Theory, Culture & Society* 12(4): 97–107. https://doi.org/10.1177/026327695012004007.

———. 2008. 'On Disappearance', in *Jean Baudrillard*. Abingdon: Routledge, pp. 40–45.

Baudrillard, Jean, and Marie Maclean. 1985. 'The Masses: The Implosion of the Social in the Media'. *New Literary History* 16(3): 577–89. https://doi.org/10.2307/468841.

Beller, J., 2021. *The World Computer: Derivative Conditions of Racial Capitalism*. Durham, NC: Duke University Press.

Borch, C. and B.T. Knudsen. 2013. 'Postmodern Crowds: Re-Inventing Crowd Thinking.' *Distinktion: Scandinavian Journal of Social Theory* 14(2): 109–113.

Boyd, Dana. 2010. 'Social Network Sites as Networked Publics: Affordances, Dynamics, and Implications', in Z. Papacharisi (ed.), *A Networked Self*. Abingdon: Routledge, pp. 47–66.

Bratton, Benjamin H. 2015. 'The Stack'. *The Log* 35: 128–59.

———. 2016. *The Stack: On Software and Sovereignty.* Cambridge, MA: MIT Press.

Bucher, Taina. 2012. 'Want to Be on the Top? Algorithmic Power and the Threat of Invisibility on Facebook'. *New Media & Society* 14(7): 1164–80. https://doi.org/10.1177/1461444812440159.

Caliskan, Koray 2020. 'Data Money: The Socio-technical Infrastructure of Cryptocurrency Blockchains'. *Economy and Society* 49(4): 540–61. https://doi.org/10.1080/03085147.2020.1774258.

Callon, Michel, Latour. Bruno, 1981. 'Unscrewing the Big Leviathan: How Actors Macro-structure Reality and How Sociologists Help Them to Do So', in K. Knorr and A. Cicourel (eds), *Advances in Social Theory and Methodology* (with Michel Callon). London: Routledge & Kegan Paul, pp. 277–303.

Calvão, F. and M. Archer. 2021. 'Digital Extraction: Blockchain Traceability in Mineral Supply Chains'. *Political Geography* 87: https://doi.org/10.1016/j.polgeo.2021.102381.

Calvão, Filipe. 2019. 'Crypto Miners: Digital Labor and the Power of Blockchain Technology'. *Economic Anthropology* 6(1): 123–34. https://doi.org/10.1002/sea2.12136.

Chun, W.H.K. 2016. *Updating to Remain the Same: Habitual New Media*. Cambridge, MA: MIT Press.

Deleuze, Gilles and Guattari, Félix. 2009. 'The Social Machine', in *Anti-Oedipus: Capitalism and Schizophrenia*. London: Penguin, pp. 185–93.

Dickel, S. and J.F. Schrape. 2017. 'The Logic of Digital Utopianism'. *NanoEthics* 11: 47–58.

Dodd, N. 2012. 'Simmel's Perfect Money: Fiction, Socialism and Utopia in *The Philosophy of Money*'. *Theory, Culture & Society* 29(7–8): 146–76.

Dodge Martin, and Rob Kitchin. 2004 'Flying through Code/Space: The Real Virtuality of Air Travel'. *Environment and Planning A* 36(2): 195–211. https://doi.org/10.1068/a3698.

DuPont, Quinn. 2017. 'Experiments in Algorithmic Governance: A History and Ethnography of "the DAO", a Failed Decentralized Autonomous Organization'. *Bitcoin and beyond*: 157–77.

———. 2019. *Cryptocurrencies and Blockchains*. Hoboken, NJ: John Wiley & Sons.

Foucault, Michel. 1977. *Discipline and Punish: The Birth of the Prison*. London: Allen Lane.

Hayes, Adam 2019. 'The Socio-technological Lives of Bitcoin'. *Theory, Culture & Society* 36(4): 49–72. https://doi.org/10.1177/0263276419826218.

Hoffman, Michael R., Luis Daniel Ibáñez and Elena Simperl. 2020. 'Toward a Formal Scholarly Understanding of Blockchain-Mediated Decentralization: A Systematic Review and a Framework'. *Frontiers in Blockchain* 3: 35. https://doi.org/10.3389/fbloc.2020.00035.

Jarvis, Craig 2022. 'Cypherpunk Ideology: Objectives, Profiles, and Influences (1992–1998)'. *Internet Histories* 6(3): 315–42. https://doi.org/10.1080/24701475.2021.1935547.

Kaplan, D.M. 2006. 'Paul Ricoeur and the Philosophy of Technology'. *Journal of French and Francophone Philosophy* 16(1–2): 42–56.

———. 'What Things Still Don't Do'. *Human Studies* 32(2): 229–240.

Kellner, Douglas. 1989. 'Boundaries and Borderlines: Reflection on Jean Baudrillard and Critical Theory.' *Current Perspectives in Social Theory* 9(1): 5–22.

Kenney, Martin, and John Zysman. 2016. 'The Rise of the Platform Economy'. *Issues in Science and Technology* 32(3): 61–69.

Labrecque, Lauren I., Jonas vor dem Esche, Charla Mathwick, Thomas P. Novak and Charles F. Hofacker. 2013. 'Consumer Power: Evolution in the Digital Age'. *Journal of Interactive Marketing* 27(4): 257–69. https://doi.org/10.1016/j.intmar.2013.09.002.

Latour, Bruno. 1990. 'Technology is Society Made Durable'. *The Sociological Review* 38(S1): 103–31. https://doi.org/10.1111/j.1467-954X.1990.tb03350.x.

———. 2007. *Reassembling the Social: An Introduction to Actor-Network-Theory*. Oxford: Oxford University Press.

Lustig, Caitlin and Nardi, Bonnie. 2015. 'Algorithmic Authority: The Case of Bitcoin'. *IEEE*: 743–52. https://ieeexplore.ieee.org/document/7069744.

Lessig, L. 2006. *Code*. New York: Basic Books.

Lycett, Mark 2013. '"Datafication": Making Sense of (Big) Data in a Complex World'. *European Journal of Information Systems* 22(4): 381–86. https://doi.org/10.1057/ejis.2013.10.

Mackenzie, Adrian. 2006. *Cutting Code: Software and Sociality*. New York: Peter Lang.

Maurer, B. 2012. 'Mobile Money: Communication, Consumption and Change in the Payments Space'. *Journal of Development Studies* 48(5): 589–604.

———. 2017. 'Blockchains Are a Diamond's Best Friend', in Nina Bandelj, Frederick F. Wherry and Viviana A. Zelizer (eds), *Money Talks: Explaining How Money Really Works*. Princeton: Princeton University Press, pp. 215–29.

McLuhan, M. 1964. 'Media Hot and Cold', in *Understanding Media: The Extensions of Man*. New York: McGraw Hill, pp. 22–32.

Morozov, E. 2013. *To Save Everything, Click Here: The Folly of Technological Solutionism*. New York: PublicAffairs.

Nakamoto, Satoshi. 2008. 'Bitcoin: A Peer-to-Peer Electronic Cash System'. *Decentralized Business Review*: 1–9.

Patterson, Dennis. 1990. 'Law's Pragmatism: Law as Practice and Narrative'. *Virginia Law Review* 76(5): 937–96. https://doi.org/10.2307/1073154.

Plantin, Jean-Christophe, and Gabriele De Seta. 2019. 'WeChat as Infrastructure: The Techno-nationalist Shaping of Chinese Digital Platforms'. *Chinese Journal of Communication* 12(3): 257–73. https://doi.org/10.1080/17544750.2019.1572633.

Qiu, Tianyi, Ruidong Zhang and Yuan Gao. 2019. 'Ripple vs. SWIFT: Transforming Cross Border Remittance Using Blockchain Technology'. *Procedia Computer Science* 147: 428–34. https://doi.org/10.1016/j.procs.2019.01.260.

Rella, Ludovico. 2020. 'Steps towards an Ecology of Money Infrastructures: Materiality and Cultures of Ripple'. *Journal of Cultural Economy* 13(2): 236–49. https://doi.org/10.1080/17530350.2020.1711532.

Ricoeur, Paul. 1971. 'The Model of the Text: Meaningful Action Considered as a Text'. *Hermeneutics and Critical Theory* 38(1): 316–33. https://www.jstor.org/stable/40970072.

———. 1980. 'Narrative Time'. *Critical Inquiry* 7(1): 169–190. https://doi.org/10.1086/448093.

———. 1983. *Time and Narrative – Volume 1*, Kathleen McLaughlin and David Pellauer (eds). Chicago: University of Chicago Press.

———. 1985. *Time and Narrative – Volume 2*, Kathleen McLaughlin and David Pellauer (eds). Chicago: University of Chicago Press.

———. 1988. *Time and Narrative: Volume 3*, Kathleen McLaughlin and David Pellauer (eds). Chicago: University of Chicago Press.

———. 2004. *Memory, History, Forgetting*, Kathleen Blamey and David Pellauer (eds). Chicago: University of Chicago Press.
———. 2014. 'The Later Wittgenstein and the Later Husserl on Language'. *Études Ricoeuriennes/Ricoeur Studies* 5(1): 28–48. https://doi.org/10.5195/errs.2014.245.
Riva, Guiseppe, and Carlo Galimberti. 1997. 'The Psychology of Cyberspace: A Socio-cognitive Framework to Computer-Mediated Communication'. *New Ideas in Psychology* 15(2): 141–58. https://doi.org/10.1016/S0732-118X(97)00015-9.
Simmel, Georg. 1971. *On Individuality and Social Forms*, Donald N. Levine (ed.). Chicago: University of Chicago Press.
———. 2004. *The Philosophy of Money*. London: Routledge.
———. 2009 [1908]. *Sociology: Inquiries into the Construction of Social Forms* (2 vols), Anthony J. Blasi, Anton K. Jacobs and Matthew Kanjiranthinkal (trans. and ed.). Leiden: Brill.
Simondon, Gilbert. 2017. *On the Mode of Existence of Technical Objects*. Minneapolis: Univocal Publishing.
Simondon, Gilbert, Ninian Mellamphy and John Hart. 1980. *On the Mode of Existence of Technical Objects*. London, Canada: University of Western Ontario.
Swartz, Lana 2020. *New Money: How Payment Became Social Media*. New Haven: Yale University Press.
Toffler, Alvin. 1980. *The Third Wave*. New York: Morrow.
Tsavelis, Dimitrios. 2023. 'The Social Consequences of the Datafication of Money: From Digital Payment Systems to Blockchain', Ph.D. dissertation. London: King's College London.
Wajcman, Judy. 2008. 'Life in the Fast Lane? Towards a Sociology of Technology and Time'. *British Journal of Sociology* 59(1): 59–77. https://doi.org/10.1111/j.1468-4446.2007.00182.x.
Wright, Aaron, and Primavera de Filippi. 2015. 'Decentralized Blockchain Technology and the Rise of *Lex Cryptographia*'. https://dx.doi.org/10.2139/ssrn.2580664.
Ziada, Hazem. 2020. 'The Digital Crowd'. *Architecture and Culture* 8(3–4): 653–66. https://doi.org/10.1080/20507828.2020.1794419.
Zuboff, S. 1988. *In the Age of the Smart Machine: The Future of Work and Power*. New York: Basic Books, Inc.

Gambling Crowds as Crypto-oracles?
Bridging the Real and the Blockchain through Utopian Markets and Oracular Shenanigans

Anthony J. Pickles

Introduction

Cryptocurrencies and gambling are intertwined. For one thing, there is the sheer volume of speculative investment in Bitcoin and the like. Fantastic rises and precipitous falls in the value of cryptocurrencies and other blockchain-based commercial offerings would be enough for many to write these markets off as idle speculation and its investors as gamblers (Rogers 2021). I did just that when visiting family over the Christmas period in 2020. Two of my relatives (neither with any experience in trading but some in gambling) were discussing their various cryptocurrency investments in the manner of day-traders (Zaloom 2006), pulling out patterns from a screen of trend lines and raw numbers. Couple this aura of speculation with the ethereality of the technology and it is easy to dismiss crypto-trading as a classic economic bubble, where fortunes appear to rest upon little more than a bet on red or black. More cynical yet, the common understanding that cryptocurrencies are dominated by wealthy 'whales' who 'pump and dump' stocks by promoting them and then offloading them puts one in mind of video-slots. In these, what you see and interpret on screen is a positively distorted representation of the mechanistic algorithm that chugs away behind the scenes, metronomically draining your balance (Schüll 2012).

Another, less well-publicised reason why cryptocurrencies intersect with gambling is that the blockchain facilitates unregulated gambling. Gambling with cryptocurrency as stakes is not a phenomenon of cryptocurrencies in the same way that speculation on cryptocurrencies is; rather, cryptocurrencies simply enable internet gambling sites to skirt round local regulations. The fact that one is using a cryptocurrency to transact is incidental and potentially a hindrance to bettors, not least because the volatility of cryptocurrencies can end up surpassing the profits and losses of gambling with them. This is a speculation on my part, but I would wager that most punters would prefer to use state-issued currency if they were allowed to gamble with it in their jurisdictions. Regardless, when many cryptocurrency users are using it just so that they can gamble, the association leaves a residue.

This chapter focuses on a third way in which gambling and cryptocurrencies are intertwined, one intimately connected to the nature of the blockchain itself. Gambling can be used as a form of common-world-building. The creation of an accepted reality is a concern peculiar to cryptocurrency enthusiasts and to potential investors who are anxious about volatility. Crypto enthusiasts are well known for their resistance to centralized authority and its prescriptive truth, but this leaves a problematic lack of consensus that threatens the real-world translatability of cryptocurrency value. Crypto enthusiasts see this as a challenge: how to establish an authoritative version of events that can be used to arbitrate disputes? Some consider platforms known as crypto-oracles, crypto prediction markets or decentralised prediction markets as the solution to anchoring the anarchic crypto crowd within a shared reality, and it all works through gambling. This chapter explains the problem and its perceived solution with recourse to theories of crowd dynamics.

The appropriateness of 'crowd' as a descriptor for what people with common interests do online depends on the extent to which the people within it consider themselves bonded in terms of their proximity, aims and movements, and whether they exhibit signs of disorder (Lee 2017: 84–85). This chapter describes online crowds of gamblers, whose individuals are acutely aware and thoughtful about the nature of the crowd of which they are part and reflect actively on their relationship to it. This is after all how gamblers choose their betting strategy – by comparing their reckoning with those of the rest of the crowd and deciding whether the price the crowd has settled on is too high or too low. The discussion here examines how this deeply individualistic approach to crowd participation has developed into a portal for engaging the real in a 'trustless' system.

Betting Exchanges and Dual Crowds

In order to understand crypto-prediction markets, it helps to be familiar with betting exchanges, the biggest of which is called Betfair Exchange. This technology is effectively the proof of concept underwriting all the current efforts to launch decentralized prediction markets. A betting exchange is a marketplace where two punters (a UK-English term meaning a person who gambles) can bet against each other at whatever odds they agree. One opts to be the bookie, i.e. the one against the outcome, and one is the punter, betting for it. To animate the technicalities, here is a hypothetical example.

I think you the reader are fantastically intelligent, charismatic and astute, and are quite a good outside bet to become the next Prime Minister of the United Kingdom. I want to stake £10 at 200 to 1, so I put an order in on the betting exchange committing to that bet. The editor of this volume then comes along and while they like you and respect your acumen, they don't think you are on a path towards the top job in UK politics, even at odds of 200 to 1. They see my order of £10 at 200 to 1, which, as the bookie, would commit them to paying out £2,000 if you become the next Prime Minister, but he takes the £10 if you do not. The editor decides to agree, 'matching' my bet.

This is essentially a contract and, like some other contracts, it can be bought or sold at different prices. Let's say you have recently been recognized with an award and there is a real buzz about you in Westminster. Other people are now betting on you at odds that have shortened to 50 to 1. Still, I am beginning to get cold feet; I now think that the previous reader is a stronger candidate than you and that others will soon realize this too, so I think your odds will probably lengthen again. I could decide to capitalize on what I see as a temporary shortening of your odds, become a bookie and take other people's bets at the new odds. This means I now win £2,000 if you become the next Prime Minister on my original bet and lose £500 at the same time on my second bet. If you do not succeed this time, then I lose my initial £10 bet and win my second £10 bet. By taking up the opposite side of this second contract at shorter odds, I have traded my way to a substantial profit if you are the next Prime Minister and no liabilities if it does not happen.

If circumstances cut the other way – say the big award goes to another reader and no one is talking about you in Westminster – then I can cut my losses in the same way by acting as bookie for the longer odds that are now available, thereby losing less money than I would if I just stuck with my original bet.

An advantage of trading in this way is that if your liabilities even out across your bets on a market, you can get your stake back quickly and put it to use in another market. In the political markets offered in the United States, this kind of trading is made more intuitive because you simply trade shares in the different outcomes. You buy a contract that pays out $1 if it comes to fruition, $0 if it does not, and then you trade those contracts at whatever price you think it deserves. Once a market is set up, a crowd emerges that takes different positions on the likelihood of the outcome. The result being a dynamic price that responds to events. In *Crowds and Power*, Canetti notes the way in which crowds on the street emerge as a product of opposing crowd-consciousnesses:

> The surest, and often the only, way by which a crowd can preserve itself lies in the existence of a second crowd to which it is related. Whether the two crowds confront each other as rivals in a game, or as a serious threat to each other, the sight, or simply the powerful image of the second crowd, prevents the disintegration of the first.
> . . . Given that they are about equal in size and intensity, the two crowds keep each other alive. (1978 [1960]: 63)

In gambling markets these opposing crowds are necessary. Markets fail and are voided if there is illiquidity on one side of the ledger. The crowd's numbers are brought level not in the numbers of people on both sides, but through currency as a representation of confidence in the opinion. Moreover, the strength of conviction is quantitatively visible in the form of the odds that each crowd is willing to back and lay on any given market.

One important clarification is that a person may feel intensely that your odds of becoming Prime Minister are shorter than 200 to 1, but may be just as vehement that your odds are longer than 50 to 1. These are not, for the most part, ideologically opposed crowds. Their opposition is over the proper interpretation of existing patterns, structures and trends. The crowds on one side of a bet and on another are likely to recompose back and forth as the odds move from one day to another. Furthermore, because political markets (such as who will be the next Prime Minister) could remain unresolved for months or years, the consensus can change considerably over that period. There are profits to be made in backing outsiders early on, but equally the composition of the opposing crowds will likely shift many times before a resolution. Market participants debate and consider options across WhatsApp groups, Twitter and on dedicated chat areas on specialist websites, thrashing out the relevant inputs and their correct weighting. These are therefore not two opposing crowds, but a dual crowd united around a single price and yet always in mutual opposition.

Prediction Markets

Betting exchanges are the platforms upon which the majority of political gambling happens these days. Prediction markets are the next step on our journey towards understanding crypto-oracles because prediction markets rest upon political gambling, and crypto-oracles rest upon prediction markets.

Prediction markets take the idea of gambling on politics and apply it to a far broader range of outcomes. Polymarket, a leading crypto-prediction market, uses the slogan 'Bet your beliefs' and offers a range of markets under the headings 'New', 'Politics', 'Crypto', 'Pop Culture', 'Trump' and 'Business'. Topics include the weather/climate, the scarcity of various commodities and their predicted prices, and who will win *Time* magazine Person of the Year. In the United States, Kalshi, one of the tech start-ups trying to mainstream prediction markets, is selling itself as a market specifically for businesses to hedge against things that would be bad news for it. This prediction market is being sold as a new way to trade derivatives: your business depends on offshore drilling, one of the two major parties is opposed to offshore drilling, and so you bet on the party who are opposed to your business interests winning as a hedge against that party preventing you from profiting from more offshore drilling. These hedges depend upon the prediction markets being sufficiently liquid, i.e. having enough money moving around within them. The hedging strategy requires an astute set of predictors who offset those hedges and bring the market back into alignment with the true likelihood of that party coming to power. If Kalshi is successful in bringing in corporate hedges, this will lead to a large expansion in the profits possible for the professional and enthusiastic amateur gamblers with whom I work, as well as for the 'market makers', companies or individuals who provide liquidity to build and stabilize a market.

As the data on a given outcome build and the deadline for a resolution draws closer – for instance, as the votes are counted – the evidence of the impending outcome can quickly build up, and some traders scramble to escape their positions and others capitalize on their foreknowledge and release their capital for the next market opportunity. A good example of this was during the 2016 referendum on membership of the European Union in the United Kingdom. A political gambling enthusiast had posted some clever modelling on the website politicalbetting.com. The model projected how the vote tallies for individual constituencies would look if the result was a dead heat. They did this by modelling demographics and factors such as

United Kingdom Independence Party (UKIP) vote share in the most recent UK General Election. Even though results trickled in overnight, this piece of modelling enabled some gamblers to conclude around 11.30 pm that an upset was very likely because the first few results to be announced appeared to indicate a higher-than-expected proportion voting to leave. They pounced. The likelihood of a Leave vote climbed precipitously, and a great deal of money was won and lost before the outcome was announced. The argument goes that if the market question is framed well, the market will converge upon an outcome that aligns with real-world events, effectively resolving itself. This means that, in theory, the betting exchange provider never needs to ever take a position on what happened themselves; all they need to do is to mark the point when consensus exceeds the threshold of agreement.

There are times when an outcome is disputed, such as the 2020 US presidential election, when the incumbent, Donald Trump, lost the election but claimed that the election had been fraudulent. At these times, it is necessary for a betting exchange provider to intervene and decide the result or to void the market and return the stakes. It is here where the distinction between betting exchanges and some crypto-prediction markets is most clearly a reflection of the ideology and structural constraints of the latter.

Decentralized Prediction Markets

When I read the call for papers about crowd dynamics on the blockchain, my point of reference was *The Wisdom of Crowds* by the journalist James Surowiecki (2005), which is the Ur-text for nonacademics interested in prediction markets. Surowiecki's book turned heads by arguing that, given the right incentives, crowds make better decisions than individuals, even individuals who are experts. In a sentence, the more diversity there is within a market, the greater its decision-making capacity when aggregated because the mistakes balance each other out and the insight converges on a single outcome. Surowiecki claims that the best way to bring this diversity together is usually through anonymous trading on a market, thereby avoiding some of the herding dynamics that occur when humans encounter one another.[1]

Whether or not prices in prediction markets represent real probabilities is vigorously debated among the community and in academic literature (e.g. Brown et al. 2019; Buckley 2017; Pathak et al. 2015). Nevertheless, the idea that they approximate real probabilities is crucial for the format's utility in the crypto community. Polymarket (launched in 2020) and Augur (version 2 launched in 2021) are Etheruem-based 'decentralized prediction markets'. Here is a taste of the questions which members of the Polymarket community are trading on at the time of writing: 'Will income taxes rise for the highest tax bracket in 2022?' (no trading at 87 cents a share); 'Will Russia expand its number of federal subjects by July 1, 2022?' (no is 96 cents a share); 'Will @realDonaldTrump tweet again by July 1st?' (no is at 98 cents a share); 'Will Jurassic World Dominion score 70% or higher Tomatometer Score?' (no is trading at 99 cents there). Notice the very high value of one position in these markets. This represents a high degree of consensus that something will happen one way and not another. The key to decentralized prediction markets as oracles is that this consensus *is* the resolution to the event.[2]

One of the primary issues on the blockchain is anchoring the chain to the physical universe to make conversions of value between them reliable and generally agree some facts. Another concern is resisting centralization, and these concerns are thought to be in tension. This enthusiastic blogger thinks that decentralized prediction markets can bridge and resolve both issues without compromises:

> At the end of the limit the outcome of an event must be reported. In the past, this was usually reported by the people who ran the prediction market itself (and you had to trust them to report correctly). With a decentralized system you can swap this out for various systems. A market for an event can have one person decide.
> If this person is trusted, then liquidity will come. If they are not, then multiple persons can report an outcome (where 2 of 3 need to agree, for example). Market participants can vote for who they want to report as well. Systems such as Augur has a token system where those who hold the token, vote on outcomes as a crowd.
> ... Finally, and perhaps the most interesting, is that all you need is a threat of an outcome for the market converge to the right outcome [sic]. The closer to the time an event comes, the more it starts to converge to the actual outcome as clarity increases. Thus, in a way, the tokens become worth zero on the one side and 1 on the other, automatically resolving itself. In a scenario where this actually ended up wrong, users can put up a deposit to dispute it: which results in arbitrator [sic] that has to come in and decide. (De la Rouviere 2015)

The markets arbitrate most decisions, enabling consensus to form on what is happening in the world without a vested authority dictating which perspective is correct.

Earlier I mentioned the 2020 US presidential election, which is an example of when a consensus was not forthcoming, and this blogger sets their sights on an arbitrator as the solution. However, a more complex, more thoroughly decentralized solution is offered in the 'white paper' released by Augur (Peterson et al. 2018), which proposes a 'forking universes' solution.

According to the White Paper's abstract:

> Augur's incentive structure is designed to ensure that honest, accurate reporting of outcomes is always the most profitable option for Reputation token holders. Token holders can post progressively-larger Reputation bonds to dispute proposed market outcomes. If the size of these bonds reaches a certain threshold, Reputation splits into multiple versions, one for each possible outcome of the disputed market; token holders must then exchange their Reputation tokens for one of these versions. Versions of Reputation which do not correspond to the real-world outcome will become worthless, as no one will participate in prediction markets unless they are confident that the markets will resolve correctly. Therefore, token holders will select the only version of Reputation which they know will continue to have value: the version that corresponds to reality. (Ibid.: 2018: 1)

Augur's developers envisage disputed versions of events that fork into entirely separate universes from the original, genesis universe. When a market forks – for instance, if enough people dispute the 2020 US presidential election outcome – new universes are created. Forking creates a new child universe for each possible outcom: one where Joe Biden won and one where Donald Trump won.

The genesis universe freezes at this point, no new markets can be created within it and a gambler cannot cash out in the genesis universe; they must cash out in one of the child universes. Therefore, the markets and the gamblers must migrate to one of the child universes. It is not possible to migrate Reputation tokens between sibling universes, as inheritance rules prohibit it. Everybody is therefore forced to take a position on which universe is valid (Peterson et al. 2018: 6). After a period of time, the universe which has the most Reputation tokens is declared the winner.[3]

In this way Augur aims to solve the issue of adherence to reality through crowd-sourced consensus, without trust or with a minimum of trust. This is an apparently 'trustless' consensus decision. The apparent value of this system is to anchor crypto to real markets and thus to stabilize its fluctuations. However, once this is achieved, the possibilities are apparently very broad.

Oracular Shenanigans

New utopic frontiers bubble up in the minds of crypto enthusiasts, such as the following from the blog entry already quoted:

> How does one build ways to incentivise these new organisations (financial gain) & how do you help it make decisions? You use prediction markets. Just as these hashtag organisations move like crowds do, so should its decision making. As the organisation goes about its goals, various outcomes are constantly generated, upon which the people in the organisation and those outside of it, bet on the outcomes, leading it automatically towards outcomes which serve the goals of the organisation. (De la Rouviere 2015)

Here, using the language of crowds, the blogger envisages prediction markets as the decision-making mechanism of an online crowd, thus magnifying its potential for real-world impact. Since its inception, the internet of things has cascaded into our homes and big data have poured into the hands of companies and governments. The blogger imagines a world in which one bets on the success of the coffee shop you frequent, and our toasters send data to bots that micro-bet on the supply of wheat based on what they know of your toast consumption. Our entire economic and political landscape is transformed through betting.

The starting point and the end goal, potentially, is 'futarchy', a term coined by the economist Robin Hanson in 2000 and one that is at the heart of crypto-utopian ideas of governance. Hanson posted a manifesto on George Mason University's website:

> In futarchy, democracy would continue to say what we want, but betting markets would now say how to get it. That is, elected representatives would formally define and manage an after-the-fact measurement of national welfare, while market speculators would say which policies they expect to raise national welfare. The basic rule of government would be:
> When a betting market clearly estimates that a proposed policy would increase expected national welfare, that proposal becomes law.
> Futarchy is intended to be ideologically neutral; it could result in anything from an extreme socialism to an extreme monarchy [a minimal state run according to libertarian theory], depending on what voters say they want, and on what speculators think would get it for them.

A few blockchain-based organizations have been working towards instituting this system of decision making for themselves and have attempted to sell such a platform to companies, all the while talking up the possibilities for futarchy at the level of the nation state.[4] One of my interviewees, a UK civil servant and an active participant on the reputation-token based Metaculus forecasting site, boldly predicted a future in which a single nation state will implement a system of governance based on prediction markets. This system would then be so successful that most other nation states would quickly follow suit, leading to a transformational change in how the world governs itself.

The specific appeal of futarchy for blockchain organizations is to harness what the community supposes to be a highly heterogenous crowd of users and owners, and turn these into an effective means of self-governance. Furthermore, in the case of Augur, the system of governance is radically decentralized, precisely because prediction markets are not resolved when *CNN* calls the election in favour of one candidate, but when the Augur trading community's financial interests reach a consensus that the call is correct. In the process, futarchy simultaneously narrows what crowds can be because they must always be gamblers on either side of a bet, and expands the importance of crowds by extending the range of activities that one can perceive through the prism of the gambling crowd.

Conclusion: Bubble-Works

This chapter examined a specific subtheme of crowding behaviour: the apparently anarchic quality of crowds on the blockchain. 'Trustless' blockchain crowding appears swamped by crazes and unpredictable self-generated dynamics. I have described crypto-prediction markets as attempts to curtail or harness that turmoil, while retaining the apparently essential quality of 'trustlessness'.

It occurs to me in the summing-up that the perceived dynamics of crowd theory, cryptocurrencies and prediction markets share the metaphor of bubbles. Cryptocurrencies are very often seen as a lather of interconnected speculative bubbles, and the interrogation and bursting of bubbles of common wisdom within prediction markets are a key strategic asset for participants in these markets. According to crowd theory, crowds are considered amorphous and disconnected, and lacking the goal orientation of a network. In the open form described by Canetti (1978 [1960]: 17), crowds they too froth and lather uncontrollably until bubbles of closed crowds form. These closed bubbles may float away or break apart within the froth again.

Despite this chaotic image, another branch of theory and a small corner of the economy think that the crowd creates wisdom of a sort (a predicted outcome) assuming a proper filter and incentivization. The filter can be a predictive question: who will be the next Attorney General of California? And opinions can be very diverse while coming up with a valuable aggregate answer. The incentive that underwrites interest in this project is personal gain. Everybody wants to win, or to hedge and win elsewhere. Intertwining financial incentive with accurate prediction and reporting thereby anchors cryptocurrencies to real-world events.

The potency of this idea has led to imaginative extrapolations (or thought bubbles) where you bet on your favourite coffee shop being successful as well as buying coffee there, so that you are financially rewarded. Taken to this extreme, the diversity of opinion that is so vaulted among those who subscribe to the efficient markets, wisdom of crowds or futarchy point of view is severely curtailed by the incentives themselves. The reality as I have observed it is a crowd that is hyperaware of itself as being a crowd. Its members are engaged in a constant process of metamorphosis in reaction against the assumed consensus thinking within the crowd, in the pursuit of profit at the expense of the crowd itself. Therefore, the resulting crowd is full of cunning thinking, but is anti-revolutionary by design, an amalgamation of maximizing individuals whose sharpest insights are intellectually flattened by the profit motive. The crowd's revolutionary potential and natural force is thereby muted and co-opted. I argue that crypto-prediction markets are both structurally inventive and curiously lacking in imagination because they all settle on markets as their arbiters, in the mould of the economist Friedrich Hayek. This paucity of imagination flattens what revolutionary potential may have existed in the new technology.

It is therefore fair to say that crypto-prediction markets sit squarely within the lineage of countercultural reactionary thinking outlined in the Introduction to this volume. Communalism through fragmentation is built into the structure of crypto-prediction markets in a manner that lashes together communities' moral and economic roles into a single ideologically pragmatic package that promises to realize the iconoclastic fantasy of trustless community. Crypto-prediction markets may yet prove themselves to be powerful tools in the crypto space, but my observations suggest that adoption has been sluggish. The limiting factor appears to be a lack of interest and a corresponding lack of liquidity, thereby indicating a deficiency of conviction in the legitimacy and potency of the platforms themselves. Achieving futarchy requires that cryptocurrency users buy in to the platform, but the absence of a crowd large enough to create efficient markets on the platforms prevents the markets from achieving the community-building effects their builders envisage. I conclude that, at present, believers in futarchy live in a bubble of sorts, even among crypto enthusiasts. The ideology of cryptocurrency enthusiasts is self-evidently pro-market, but, like most of the rest of us, the community at large remain justifiably cautious about delegating matters of truth and reality to the invisible hand.

Anthony J. Pickles is Assistant Professor in Social Anthropology at the University of Birmingham. His most recent book is *Money Games: Gambling in a Papua New Guinea Town* (Berghahn Books, 2019).

Notes

1. Borch (2007) refutes this thesis by pointing out that in crowd theory, actors are neither rational nor irrational and that when they are aggregated, their actions are a dynamic that exceeds the dichotomy.
2. To be frank, my fieldwork is based almost entirely in the UK legal betting exchanges and my knowledge of other exchanges is at a background level. I am not an expert in this community and I am going by their self-description here.
3. It is possible to wait until a winner is declared and then migrate your tokens to the winning universe after the fact.
4. See https://www.youtube.com/watch?v=XonwBPXpyJQ 2018 (last accessed 29 September 2023).

References

Borch, Christian. 2007. 'Crowds and Economic Life: Bringing an Old Figure Back in'. *Economy and Society* 36(4): 549–73.

Brown, Alisdair, J. James Reade and Leighton Vaughan Williams. 2019. 'When Are Prediction Market Prices Most Informative?' *International Journal of Forecasting* 35(1): 420–28.

Buckley, Peter, 2017. 'Evidencing the Forecasting Performance of Predication Markets: An Empirical Comparative Study'. *Journal of Prediction Markets* 11(2): 60–76.

Canetti, Elias. 1978 [1960]. *Crowds and Power*, Carol Stewart (trans.). New York: Continuum Publishing Corporation.

De la Rouviere, Simon. 2015. 'Why & How Decentralized Prediction Markets Will Change Just about Everything.'. Retrieved 19 August 2023 from https://medium.com/@ConsenSys/why-how-decentralized-prediction-markets-will-change-just-about-everything-15ff02c98f7c#.kx6yj73jl.

Lee, Raymond. 2017. 'Do Online Crowds Really Exist? Proximity, Connectivity and Collectivity'. *Distinktion: Journal of Social Theory* 18(1): 82–94.

Pathak, Deepak, David Rothschild and Miroslav Dudik. 2015. 'A Comparison of Forecasting Methods: Fundamentals, Polling, Prediction Markets, and Experts'. *Journal of Prediction Markets* 9(2): 1–31.

Peterson, Jack, Joseph Krug, Micah Zoltu, Austin K. Williams and Stephanie Alexander (Forecast Foundation). 2018. 'Augur: A Decentralized Oracle and Prediction Market Platform'. Retrieved 4 September 2023 from https://arxiv.org/abs/1501.01042.

Rogers, Gayle. 2021. *Speculation: A Cultural History from Aristotle to AI*. New York: Columbia University Press.

Schüll, Natasha. 2012. *Addiction by Design*. Princeton: Princeton University Press.

Surowiecki, James. 2005. *The Wisdom of Crowds*. New York: Anchor.

Tech Open Air. 2018. 'What Is Futarchy? – Trading on The Future – Friederike Ernst #TOA18'. Retrieved 19 August 2023 from https://www.youtube.com/watch?v=XonwBPXpyJQ 2018.

Zaloom, Caitlyn. 2006. *Out of the Pits: Traders and Technology from Chicago to London*. Chicago: University of Chicago Press.

Affective Processes in Cryptocurrency Markets
An Exploration with Crowd Theory

Anna Vennonen

Introduction

Cryptocurrencies are renowned for their dramatic price movements. Yet, there is still much to learn about the social forces driving this volatility beyond the commonly invoked dichotomy of fear and greed, which ebbs and flows with the 'sentiment of the masses'. There is a long tradition of attempting to understand and predict public sentiment from an economic perspective, through content analysis and theories of 'herding behaviour' (Ahmad 2011: 89). The latter can be defined as 'the tendency of investors to suppress their own beliefs and their private information in favour of the market consensus when trading individual assets' (Philippas et al. 2020: 2). Herding behaviour has been associated with conditions of high volatility (Blasco et al. 2012; Tan et al. 2008), making cryptocurrency markets a prime setting for it to occur.

Economists have demonstrated herding behaviour to influence cryptocurrency prices (Poyser 2018), with social imitation increasing as a sense of 'uncertainty' rises (Bouri et al. 2019). Analysis of price dynamics reveals heterogeneous crowding dynamics, indicating both trend-chasing and contrarian behaviours (King and Koutmos 2021). Researchers have also pointed to the role of social media in shaping today's financial markets (Ajjoub et al. 2021). This may be particularly pronounced in the case of digitally native cryptocurrency, which lacks the offline establishments of traditional finance, prompting users to seek information about their financial choices in the porous, networked environments of the internet. Recent research examining this relationship has identified significant increases in trading volumes for Bitcoin and *memecoin* Dogecoin following Twitter posts by key influencer Elon Musk (Ante 2021).

Together these findings point to affectively charged groups in the cryptocurrency scene, with multiple approaches, agendas and leaders. *Affect* refers to the power to affect and to be affected by the world around us. The literature on affect brings our attention to the complex correspondence of the mind, body, thought and emotion, and their relationships with other bodies, matter and technology (Clough 2008). Researchers in digital media studies have recently highlighted affect as a key consideration for online interaction (Coleman 2018; Ringrose and Mendes 2018) and have called for studies that pay attention to how affect is experienced and transmitted online (Sampson et al. 2018; Stage 2013). This chapter explores the presence of affective processes in cryptocurrency markets and its social 'scenes' by applying revised crowd theory. It considers what a perspective on crowds may reveal about the social factors mediating people's behaviour in these contemporary settings, while contributing to the limited ethnographic perspectives on how these markets are experienced 'on the ground' by cryptocurrency users.

Cryptocurrency as a 'Trustless', Accessible Peer-to-Peer System

Bitcoin, the first widely adopted virtual currency using blockchain, promised a 'trustless' way to exchange value. The white paper written by the mysterious 'Satoshi Nakamoto' describes a 'fully peer-to-peer' system that renounces the need for third parties like banks to oversee transactions (Nakamoto 2008). Bitcoin achieves this by solving the 'double spending problem' of digital cash, through decentralized, proof-of-work cryptography. Pseudonymous addresses and their transactions appear publicly on the blockchain, making privacy and security a matter of personal responsibility for individuals holding private keys to an address. Trust previously placed in the legitimacy of institutions and governments is understood by its enthusiasts to have become embedded in the code itself (Maurer et al. 2013: 263). As new monies 'of the people', cryptocurrencies invoke a flattening of hierarchies through their peer-to-peer narrative (Nelms et al. 2018). Having enabled access to a diverse range of financial products, an estimated 10% of global internet users between sixteen and sixty-four years old now hold cryptocurrency (GWI 2022).

Some social scientists have challenged claims of cryptocurrency's 'trustlessness', arguing that trust remains a key factor in the survival and function of cryptocurrencies, despite narratives of blockchain as an apolitical technology capable of separating money from social life (Dodd 2018). Researchers emphasized the shared ideologies and narratives that sustain cryptocurrencies (Faria 2022) and highlighted their engagement with broader debates around money (Dodd 2018; Maurer et al. 2013), as exemplified in Nakamoto's reference to the Global Financial Crisis in Bitcoin's 'genesis block' (see Tardi 2021). The appeal of cryptocurrency is multifaceted; as Nigel Dodd writes, 'there is not one Bitcoin, but several', recognizing its many meanings, and the range of political and ideological opinions found within the loosely defined movement (Dodd 2018: 36). This alludes to the way in which motivations behind the phenomenon are more than economic, as seen in attempts to achieve different types of value on both individual and collective scales.

Following online ethnography in the South Korean Bitcoin frenzy of 2017–18, Seung Cheol Lee (2020) suggests that cryptocurrency adoption can be understood as a cultural phenomenon rather than a collection of individuals' rational economic choices. Lee (2020) argues there is no clear line between a 'rational' investor and a 'superstitious' gambler, proposing that the latter subjectivities are a response to the irrational and 'magical' qualities of the market itself, determined in self-referential and self-fulfilling ways. Lay Bitcoin users were found to express scepticism about the rationality and predictability of the market itself, perceiving even formalized tools of analysis to be inadequate to guide speculation. As Lee (2020), following Orléan (2014), points out, the prices of cryptocurrencies are in part determined not by what someone *believes* about their value, but by what they think the *majority of other people* believe. This emphasizes the social contexts of decisions, by which individuals exist in some degree of bondage to one another's sentiments (Huh et al. 2014). Considering insights from the social sciences and economists' reports of herding behaviour, exploring a link to crowd theory appears a compelling pursuit.

Crowd Theory: Classical to Contemporary

Crowd theory was popularized towards the end of the nineteenth century among social theorists in Europe and

America seeking to understand large groups of people. Industrialization had shifted the social landscape, with the birth of cities producing new masses of people living and working in close proximity. The ruling class sought ways to control these populations as traditional structures like the church, the family and the army lost significance (Reicher 2004). Theorists including Gabrielle Tarde, Gustave Le Bon and Georg Simmel became fascinated with crowds, considering them as a central human phenomenon with which we can understand society (Borch 2012).

In 1895, Le Bon published *The Crowd: A Study of the Popular Mind*. He wrote in the heyday of sociology's preoccupation with crowds when French academics saw crowds as a threat to bourgeois society (Borch and Knudsen 2013). For Le Bon, this represented 'the era of crowds': a time when the 'divine right' of the masses would replace that of kings and traditional rulers, potentially marking the end of Western civilization and a return to anarchy (Le Bon 2001 [1896]: 9). Le Bon saw crowds as groups of people that take on a 'collective mind' through shared ideas and sentiments. He theorized that this caused a temporary loss of individuals' personalities and self-consciousness, with crowds becoming more than the sum of their parts. Group sentiment was thought to overpower individual sentiments and moralities, making crowds as easily 'heroic' as 'criminal' (ibid.: 11). While other crowd theorists considered emotional affect to spread through bodily closeness (see Tarde 2010 [1969]), Le Bon also spoke of isolated individuals sharing sentiment, creating a 'psychological crowd':

> At certain moments half a dozen men might constitute a psychological crowd, which may not happen in the case of hundreds of men gathered together by accident. On the other hand, an entire nation, though there may be no vis-

ible agglomeration, may become a crowd under the action of certain influences. (Le Bon [1896] 2001: 14)

For Le Bon, the crowd was not defined by the number of participants or their physical co-presence, but, instead, by three defining characteristics: anonymity, contagion and suggestion (Le Bon 2001 [1896]: 17–18). Anonymity was thought to lead to a loss of social responsibility. Contagion was said to act as a 'hypnotic-like' order spreading sentiment among participants and causing a sacrifice of personal interests in favour of collective interest (ibid.: 12). Suggestibility described how individuals became 'unconscious' of their actions and open to external suggestions (ibid.). These suggestions, Le Bon proposed, may come from a 'crowd leader', themselves seduced by crowd sentiment and feeling its calling so deep it may lead to martyrdom (ibid.: 21). Overall, Le Bon's crowd conjures a picture of an unconscious and hypnotic mass, with no sense of individual agency: 'An individual in a crowd is a grain of sand amid other grains of sand, which the wind stirs up at will' (ibid.: 19).

This perspective dismisses people's motivations, experiences and agency, obscuring the origins of crowd sentiment. On the whole, Le Bon's work is highly critical of crowds, contrasting with more positive conceptions of crowds as offering freedom from oneself, and allowing for personal and collective transformations (Canetti 1962; Durkheim 1995 [1912]). Le Bon's work has faced a variety of criticisms, including for its racist, sexist, classicist and undemocratic features, and its overemphasis on crowds as irrational, criminal and destructive (Baker 2012; Sampson 2012; Tutenges 2015). Recognizing these issues, theorists have sought to salvage and revise some of Le Bon's ideas to explore collective behaviour.

Christian Borch calls for a revival of crowd theory to explain speculative economic activity. According to Borch, *suggestion* is the defining quality of a crowd for major theorists Le Bon and Tarde (2007: 553). Borch revisits the concept, proposing that it be understood as a *semiconscious* activity that combines aspects of 'rational' thinking with affect, desire and passion (ibid.: 550). Borch hopes to move beyond the dichotomy of rational and irrational, to arrive at a theory of behaviour that sees the integration of the two. This revised view of suggestion resolves the issue of 'unconscious' crowds, creating space for individual agency and influence. Further, Borch and Knudsen (2013) advocate a rethinking of crowd theory in light of digital media, to update classical notions of physically congregating crowds to crowding in virtual spaces. The authors highlight how digital media still involves transmissions between bodies, often in new ways to those afforded by social hierarchies established offline. This perspective then raises the question of how participants in online crowds transmit and experience sentiment without bodily presence.

While contemporary life has readily adopted casual notions of *virality* – seen in large-scale social media events, trends, memes, hashtag activism and the rise of 'influencers' over the past decade, few studies have engaged with crowd theory to examine social media. Yet in light of seemingly pervasive contemporary social media, Hayden (2021) suggests we are seeing a resurgent concern with crowding, similar to that which inspired classical crowd theory. Literature on mass social media behaviour has generally taken interest in collective action, particularly political movements (Borge-Holthoefer et al. 2014; Schroeder et al. 2014; Syndicus 2018). Among the engagement with crowd theory by Le Bon, Tarde and others, Stephanie Baker (2011, 2012) has discussed social media use in the 2011 English riots. Her work expands classical crowd theory beyond the Tardean idea of emotional contagion through physical proximity, proposing the concept of a 'mediated crowd' to account for social media use in contemporary crowds. Baker's term is helpful when looking at crowds as 'collective communities' that operate online and offline (Baker 2012). The concept of the 'mediated crowd' fits contemporary protests like the Arab Spring, though it inadequately accounts for crowding online that is not organized around offline collective action.

Carsten Stage (2013) uses crowd theory to explore affective blogging in the case study of the *65 Red Roses* blog: a life journal of Eva Markvoort, a young woman with cystic fibrosis. Stage builds on work by Baker (2011) and Blackman (2012), theorizing three kinds of crowds: the body-to-body crowd, the mediated crowd and the *online* crowd – the latter addition describing crowding in virtual settings. Stage follows Tarde (2010 [1969]) by distinguishing between 'publics' and 'crowds'. He draws on Warner's (2002) work, which outlines three publics: (1) a social totality of the field in question (e.g. a nation); (2) a gathering of people at a common event or space (e.g. a concert); or (3) a grouping of people related to each other through texts. Stage theorizes that online spaces operate as publics most of the time and transition to crowds temporarily through shared affective processes. While publics and crowds are traditionally dichotomized, Stage sees them as mutually inclusive. This view of crowding dynamics appears to better reflect contemporary internet crowds, known for their transient and ad hoc character (Kamath and Caverlee 2011).

Applying Crowd Theory to the Cryptoscene with Ethnography

The analyses presented in this chapter are based on seven months of ethnographic research conducted online and in person in Helsinki in the first half of 2022.[1] Fieldwork consisted of participant observation among three cryptocurrency social groups. The first of these was a small online group of crypto enthusiasts who met weekly via Zoom to discuss cryptocurrency news, investing, trading and related topics. The second was a local Bitcoin community in Helsinki, which met monthly in bars to discuss Bitcoin and socialize. I sought approval from community leaders to include the groups in my study and introduced my research to members. Third, the study involved netnography (Kozinets 2010, 2015) on Reddit, particularly among the largest cryptocurrency group with 6.4 million members: r/CryptoCurrency (r/CC), entitled 'Cryptocurrency News and Discussion'. The group is open to the public, with users engaging in activities on the page pseudonymously. In addition to online and offline participant observation, I conducted thirty-three semi-structured interviews with fifteen users, with whom I obtained written informed consent. This chapter draws especially on the online fieldwork and interviews with users, mainly located in Finland and Western Europe.

Cryptocurrency is born from digital technologies and the internet. Given the amount of activity happening online around cryptocurrency, it made sense to use digital ethnography. This research method was conceived in response to the increasing prevalence of 'the digital' in everyday life. In contemporary times there is an increasing 'leakiness' between 'online' and 'offline' life, such that today many of us live in contexts that are materially, socially and sensorially entangled with digital technology (Pink et al. 2016). Nowadays online worlds have become a highly relevant area for anthropological inquiry. Digital ethnography maintains the approach of studying people in their qualitative contextual depth, adapting traditional ethnographic methods and ethical principles to online terrains (Morais et al. 2020).

Over 23,000 cryptocurrencies have been traded on the market (CoinMarketCap 2023), with users often holding multiple at a time, each with unique qualities and social followings. Most anthropological literature has focused on Bitcoin, which continues to hold market dominance. To broaden this focus to include sociality around other cryptocurrencies, I used a multisited approach (Marcus 1995), engaging with three 'sites' among the cryptoscene. This allowed for data triangulation that helped to establish contexts and verify interpretations when working with online data, which can lack social and linguistic metadata (Snodgrass 2014). A multisited approach echoes the process many cryptocurrency users themselves go through, moving between multiple settings in efforts to synthesize information. For Falzon (2009: 9), multisited ethnography can offer researchers a sense of how their interlocutors navigate their worlds in dispersed or unsettled ways. Recognizing field sites are not 'pure', 'bounded' or 'whole', these sites offered three windows into crypto sociality. Fieldsites can be described as constructed 'networks' of spaces, people and objects that get included in the study (Burrell 2009). Considering this, I wish to emphasize the vastness and diversity of the cryptoscene, into which this chapter offers merely a glimpse.

Engaging with the recent renewal of crowd theory, this chapter explores social processes that may give rise to measurable market impacts known to economists as 'herding', from an ethnographic perspective. To the author's knowledge, crowd theory has not been applied to cryptocurrency before the chapters presented by authors in this volume. My chapter aims to contribute to a preliminary base to encourage future research in this direction. Building on Stage's (2013) work, I apply crowd theory to digital media surrounding cryptocurrencies. Given the lack of physical congregation surrounding cryptocurrencies, I focus on the role of affect on social media in producing virtual crowds. In Stage's (2013) study of the *65 red roses* blog site, he traced linguistic material for representations of bodily reactions, distorted comment form and temporally simultaneous gathering around posts. Unlike Stage's blog site, affective processes in crypto communities are likely spread through a wide range of channels, making it difficult to pin down points of influence. Considering this and the multisited nature of the study, I adopted a broader approach, considering affective behaviour in relation to social processes in the scene, as observed in online forums and live sessions, and as conveyed by users in interviews.

Conceptualizing the 'Community' and the 'Crowd' in the Cryptoscene

People engage with cryptocurrencies in many different ways: mining it, trading it, developing it, investing in it, transacting with it and working in the broader industry that has formed around it. The topic of cryptocurrency has many subtopics and has given rise to many self-described communities. The concept of 'community' has been questioned by anthropologists since the 1980s for its lack of preciseness in accounting for ethnographic subjects, which now move fluidly through the physical world and online spaces, unattached to particular social locations (Kozinets 2010). As a result, terms like 'community' and 'culture' are destabilized in contemporary times (ibid.). I use the *emic* – or participants' own – casual designation of 'communities' while recognizing, as many of my participants do, that the traditional use of 'community' evokes shared values, meanings, norms and symbols that are not necessarily reflected in practice. Further, I consider Vered Amit's argument that ambiguities in the term make it 'good to think with', having the potential to reveal different concepts of sociality through the eyes of its users (Amit 2010).

Like other contemporary communities, groups in the cryptoscene emerge around shared interests, values, experiences or motivations, and support the transfer of knowledge and resources between members. Virtual communities need not have well-established societal rules and instead are held together by shared emotions, lifestyles, beliefs, experiences and practices (Cova 1997). Often blurring the lines between 'consumer' and 'participatory' cultures, the communities I joined shared, discussed and synthesized information, helping users navigate a space colloquially referred to as 'The Wild West'. Following Stage's (2013) work, I consider online communities like the Reddit page (r/CC) to be one of Warner's (2002) publics, which can produce crowd behaviour when sharing affect. While publics traditionally involved hierarchies of established institutions (e.g. media), online publics flattened this hierarchy, making the transmission of information, and therefore the creation of publics themselves, more accessible (Lünenborg 2020).

There are multiple lenses through which to identify crowds among the cryptoscene, as shown by the authors in this volume. Financial markets are widely understood to be affected by a 'crowd syndrome' (Borch 2007). Building on research that considers a relationship between online sociality and market volatility, this study has sought to better understand the formation of crowds in online communities surrounding cryptocurrencies. From the perspective of market data, human and nonhuman actors like bots and corporations form virtual crowds that move between positions of buying, selling and holding. These actors are seen to congregate and disintegrate around certain price points seen, for instance, on the live 'candlestick' charts to which many cryptocurrency users refer. However, other kinds of crowding also take place on social media and online communities adjacent to cryptocurrency markets. Being relatively new and alternative, most educational material and updates surrounding cryptocurrencies are accessed on the internet, often via online communities that provide users with an overview of current events and sentiments. Taking *suggestion* – the key premise of crowd theory according to Borch (2007) – I look at the development of crowds through the lens of affective processes happening in these communities.

Language as an Indication of Affect in the Cryptoscene

> If you hear 'To the moon!' and 'Hold the line!' regarding your coin: Sell. Run. Call your mom. Do ANYTHING except FOMO in. (Reddit user, 2021)

To begin, I would like to introduce the emic language used by market participants as an indication of affective processes with the potential to create crowds that swing markets. The cryptocurrency scene is deeply infused with internet slang and meme culture. It does not take long traversing online forums to learn terms like 'FUD' (Fear, Uncertainty and Doubt), 'FOMO' (Fear Of Missing Out), 'WAGMI' (We're All Going to Make It), 'aping in' (buying recklessly) and 'shilling' (promoting). Such terms, as demonstrated in the expression above, refer to sentiments moving about in the market, and their power to affect people's choices. Without proposing that the terms themselves cause affect, though words can do this (Röggla 2019), I focus on them as a signal for the prevalence of affective processes in these spaces.

Fear, uncertainty and doubt are common experiences among people attempting to ride the waves of volatility in the cryptocurrency market. The concept of 'FUD', adopted from the marketing industry, now appears in online discussions to acknowledge the potential for information to elicit fear, uncertainty and doubt in its audience, especially holders of particular cryptocurrencies. The spread of 'FUD' or *'fud'* can trigger sell-offs, discourage buying and cause prices to fall, further compounding the effect. This happens daily across the thousands of projects traded, sometimes affecting the whole market, appearing, for instance, as 'China Fud' or 'Fed Fud'.[2] The terms provide users with a shorthand way to acknowledge the collective emotions moving prices. Further, they express users' recognition that *words themselves* can harm markets (Lee 2020). As a Reddit user described, these emotions could spread through forums or 'subs' in viral ways: 'I avoid this sub like the plague when markets take a nosedive', the 'panic is all too contagious'. Such conditions pose a threat to the market in general, but especially to cryptocurrencies with a smaller market capitalization.

In recognizing the affective power of FUD, some communities create *anti*-FUD environments. In these settings, the act of labelling information as 'FUD' may itself direct collective sentiment. Replies like 'FUD!' and 'Fudster' can mark information as an attempt to manipulate others, advising its dismissal. At times, valid critical analysis gets dismissed too, causing users to pre-empt with 'not fud, *but . . .*' to protect their posts. In extreme cases, anti-FUD behaviour becomes censorship when page moderators delete unfavourable information, acting as silent 'crowd leaders' directing sentiment. This behaviour is commonly associated with dubious, volatile tokens known colloquially as 'sh*tcoins'. In their worst forms, these appear as scams; including 'rug pulls', Ponzi, and 'pump and dump' schemes – the latter of which may appear to have highly committed 'communities' whose members promote or 'shill' the token, urging others to 'load their bags' and 'buy the dip', only to exit through the liquidity newcomers provide, causing the price to plummet.

These groups are often described in forums like r/CC as 'cult-like' in their mission to defend their project against FUD by forming an echo chamber to protect their beliefs and interests. The term 'FUD' itself describes emotions rather than the information *causing* those emotions, allowing easy dismissal in a space that privileges notions of 'rationality' above emotions. This enables terms like 'FUD' to become tools in mediating the interpretation of, or access to, information. As a user explained, the term 'FUD' could be used to 'discredit any and all negative comments regarding [one's] favourite project/scam'. One of my interlocutors described being subjected to condemnation when playing the devil's advocate: 'I just say "hey but what if this happens?" and then straight away, there's like ten of them on you like hyenas trying to take a piece of you.' These experiences are reminiscent of Le Bon's depiction of crowds:

> The masses have never thirsted after truth. They turn aside from evidence that is not to their taste, preferring to deify error, if error seduce them. Whoever can supply them with illusions is easily their master; whoever attempts to destroy their illusions is always their victim. (Le Bon 2001 [1896]: 64)

While not all crowds behave this way, Le Bon's words resonate with some behaviour seen in the cryptoscene. Digital media affords anonymity, which may lessen a sense of social responsibility (Keipi and Oksanen 2012), while also allowing affect to reach audiences in relatively synchronized ways (Stage 2013). In the case of cryptocurrency, users are simultaneously impacted by price movements, creating mass shared experiences. These conditions hold the potential for personal interests to converge into collective ones where there are shared goals and desires, like achieving specific price points. Action towards such goals is advocated in phrases like 'buy the dip', which encourages users to buy during a market downturn, or 'diamond hands' which idealizes holding. This rhetoric can pulse through cryptocurrency forums, encouraging buys and discouraging sells through notions of togetherness, carried in terms like 'WAGMI' ('We're All Going to Make It'). These examples of affective language align with the influential role social media is recognized to play in mediating mass sentiment. This situation exhibits features of Le Bon's (1896) *psychological crowd*, conceived more than a hundred years ago. Unlike Le Bon's 'unconscious' crowds, crowds in the cryptoscene exhibit a merging of individual and collective desires, blurring the lines of 'intentional' and 'unintentional' action. Appearing to engage in relatively synchronized affective processes, these groups fit Stage's (2013) description of the online crowd.

Seeing and Resisting: The Pursuit of 'Rationality' and the Creation of an Anti-crowd

The previous section explored language as an indication of affective processes in cryptocurrency markets. This section explores how market participants relate to crowds, including by aiming to separate themselves from them. This aim is reflected in the anti-conformist ethos of cryptocurrency's roots, influenced by cypherpunks, anarchists and libertarians. Emerging amid the 2007–8 financial crisis, Bitcoin's white paper presented a new vision for 'trustless' money that allowed freedom from traditional finance, governments and corporate surveillance. In this way, the original 'crowd' of cryptocurrency could be seen as a protest. From these origins, a high value was placed on individualism, freedom, experimentation and innovation, which largely oppose the idea of being among 'the masses'. Such views are furthered by the popularization of contrarian trading strategies. As Borch (2007) highlights, these strategies draw from Le Bon's crowd theory by considering crowd sentiment as 'irrational', and therefore informing a possible 'rational' action. Together, contrarian strategies and the ideological rhetoric of individualism create a tension with the idea of crowds. Market participants not only move with crowds but also resist them.

Among people in the cryptoscene, resistance to herding is widely recognized as a foundational component of being a rational and therefore *legitimate* investor or trader (de Goede 2005). Retail investors attempt to protect themselves against manipulation by powerful actors with large holdings, colloquially referred to as 'whales', by identifying crowds and their influencers. In a live Zoom meeting with the trading and investing group, the host reading the Bitcoin chart remarked that 'the big boys are having a field day'. Another added that 'they want us to capitulate' – to succumb to fear in a falling market and sell. To avoid being caught up in these market crowds, people were encouraged to be aware of whales, avoid exposing themselves to influencers, be wary of social media and understand the forces behind price action. In forums, this sometimes took the form of 'whale watching', a practice by which members track large wallets and their transactions on the blockchain, often voluntarily producing complex reports analysing these moves.

Communities in which I participated took purposeful action to avoid crowding and unchecked influence. Herding behaviour was discouraged through formal rules created by administrators and culturally produced standards, practices, beliefs and values. Education, research and rational decision making were encouraged. These ideals are echoed in the scene's adage, 'DYOR', short for 'do your own research'. Being part of 'the masses' was often looked down upon, with 'smart money' being spoken of as early, contrarian or manipulative. The view of crowding in the cryptoscene often echoed traditional views on crowds popularized by classical crowd theory as dumb, irrational and unsuccessful (Borch 2007). Many of my participants emphasized the importance of rationality and strove to achieve it through self-education, self-discipline and self-awareness. This kind of self-development was considered fundamental in managing one's emotions in the high-risk, high-reward environment of the market that one of my interlocutors, Jason,[3] a cryptocurrency trader, described in an interview:

> I can speak from experience as somebody with tens of thousands in the game. Watching your portfolio drop 50% when you're in five figures or more is absolutely gut-wrenching. We are on a rollercoaster. You gotta have some steel to actually trade your way through that or hold through that even, without getting seriously emotional.

Perhaps the most significant way of practising more 'rational' engagement with the cryptocurrency market was through Technical Analysis (TA). The well-founded practice, originating in the nineteenth century, is grounded in the idea that human behaviour drives prices in a trend-like manner that repeats over time (Murphy 1999). These trends are revealed in patterns on charts, which can help people understand the market and make more profitable decisions. The method remains inherently subjective as the viewer identifies patterns from the data and interprets their meanings. An interlocutor of mine once described reading charts as 'looking at people's emotions'. One of the skills of a chart reader is the ability to draw insights from mass sentiment appearing in real-time while resisting the 'seductive pull' of the market (Hassoun 2005, cited in Borch 2007). As captured by Stäheli (2006) and echoed by

Borch (2007), this results in a paradox in which the rationality of the reader rests on relating to the irrationality of the crowd. If *suggestion* is a semi-conscious process, TA can be understood to involve a type of emotional-mental work to make the unconscious conscious through an exercise of self-awareness:

> When I wake up some mornings and the Asia sessions have been going on a rampage and there's green candles everywhere, I just sit on my hands, I literally sometimes sit on my hands – saying 'don't do it' – feeling the greed and the fear taking control over your common sense . . . next thing you're thinking crazy stuff . . . you're thinking 'I'll get in here, I'll put the stop loss here, I'll use a bit of leverage' . . . You've got to stop it. Shut the laptop, go off and do something else productive with your day. (Jason, cited in Vennonen 2023)

The trader's response to the chart is both *affective* – feeling greed and fear 'take over their common sense' – and *intentional* – sitting on their hands to physically block an affective response, saying 'don't do it' and disengaging from the activity altogether. As the trader describes, the affective nature of the chart can also prompt the rationalization of possible actions, such that emotion and cognition are integrated in ways that escape the false binary of 'rational' and 'irrational'. Alongside the use of multiple 'logics', people also act in response to their affective experiences of the world in ways that go beyond individual rational economizing. Borch's (2007: 550) emphasis on *suggestion* as involving a blend of 'rationality, affect, desire and passion' – also understood in terms of intentional and affective action – better accounts for the experience of relating to the crowd. Compared to classical notions of 'unconscious' crowds, this view of suggestion captures the experience of affect *and* the resistance to it. Cryptocurrency markets and financial markets more generally provide a valuable angle to study crowd dynamics, precisely because of this resistance, which is less pronounced in other crowding situations like a supportive blog site, a concert or a protest. Exploring crowding in financial contexts highlights the differing levels of intentionality and self-consciousness around crowds. This is especially important online, where being in a crowd is far less tangible. Attention to these factors is particularly relevant in the case of cryptocurrency, where many users glean information from socially rich online environments, whether intentionally or not.

As highlighted by Shapiro in the Introduction, crowds have been described as seeking expansion or stability (Canetti 1962). Comparable dynamics can be seen in the on line communities and media surrounding cryptocurrencies. Common phrases like 'to the moon', which imply a cryptocurrency will dramatically rise in value, support the fast growth of the crowd by attracting speculative actors. Likewise, spreading 'FUD' may prompt mass-selling events. As sentiments can rapidly dissipate or change direction, these crowds lack the sustainability of long-term communities to assure value, thus contributing to volatility. Ideals like rationality, discipline and holding are constructed over longer periods of time in cryptocurrency communities, cultivating stability and even helping to produce subjects that resist crowds. These ideals, together with collective understandings of value and trust, contribute to a sustained community of belief in cryptocurrencies (Vennonen 2023). Reflecting on the original curiosity that inspired these works – the simultaneous emergence of crowds that seek expansion and communities that seek stability – it seems both have played essential roles in producing the global, decade-long phenomenon we know today.

Conclusion

This chapter has explored the application of crowd theory to the social worlds surrounding cryptocurrency. In examining language from the scene, the work highlights the prevalence of affect flowing through online channels like forums, creating fertile conditions for crowds to emerge, particularly in moments of volatility and uncertainty when many people interpret and act in synchronized ways. The chapter suggests that affectively charged communications and the linguistic signals describing them influence mass sentiments. These situations are reminiscent of Le Bon's *psychological crowd* and can be interpreted through Stage's (2013) concept of the *online crowd*. The chapter has also explored the other side of the coin – how cryptocurrency users pursuing rational ideals attempt to identify and resist crowding by developing their awareness of affect. These instances of resistance are not well accounted for in classical crowd theory. Engaging with contemporary crowd theory, this chapter supports the consideration of *suggestion* as a semi-conscious process, as Borch (2007) proposes, to account for intentional and affective action exhibited by people encountering crowds.

Acknowledgements

This research was supported by Blockchain Research Lab.

Anna Vennonen recently graduated from an international master's program in contemporary societies at the University of Helsinki. Her research interests include the societal impact of emerging technologies and contemporary financial subjectivities. Her thesis explores the social construction of value in the cryptocurrency scene.

Notes

1. The research for this chapter was partially funded by Blockchain Research Lab (BRL), a nonprofit organization supporting junior scholars in blockchain-related research. BRL did not influence the study design, data collection, analysis, interpretation or writing of the results, including this chapter, or the decision to write and submit this chapter for publication. As the sole researcher, I assume full responsibility for the integrity and accuracy of the data analysis.
2. 'China Fud' has generally referred to fear, uncertainty and doubt surrounding developments in Chinese cryptocurrency regulation. Similarly, 'Fed Fud' has referred to public concern around the actions of the United States Federal Reserve (also known as 'the Fed').
3. A pseudonym.

References

Ahmad, Khurshid. 2011. 'The "Return" and "Volatility" of Sentiments: An Attempt to Quantify the Behaviour of the Markets?', in Khurshid Ahmad (ed.), *Affective Computing and Sentiment Analysis*. Dordrecht: Springer, pp. 89–99.

Ajjoub, Carl, Thomas Walker and Yunfei Zhao. 2021. 'Social Media Posts and Stock Returns: The Trump Factor'. *International Journal of Managerial Finance* 17(2): 185–213. DOI:10.1108/IJMF-02-2020-0068.

Amit, Vered. 2010. 'Community as "Good to Think with": The Productiveness of Strategic Ambiguities'. *Anthropologica* 52(2): 357–63. http://www.jstor.org/stable/29546038.

Ante, Lennart. 2021. 'How Elon Musk's Twitter Activity Moves Cryptocurrency Markets'. BRL Working Paper. Hamburg: Blockchain Research Lab.

Baker, Stephanie. 2011. 'The Mediated Crowd: New Social Media and New Forms of Rioting'. *Sociological Research Online* 16(4): 195–204. DOI:10.5153/sro.2553.

———. 2012. 'From the Criminal Crowd to the "Mediated Crowd": The Impact of Social Media on the 2011 English Riots'. *Safer Communities* 11(1): 40–49. DOI:10.1108/17578041211200100.

Blackman, Lisa. 2012. *Immaterial Bodies: Affect, Embodiment, Mediation*. London: Sage.

Blasco, Natividad, Pilar Corredor and Sandra Ferreruela. 2012. 'Does Herding Affect Volatility? Implications for the Spanish Stock Market'. *Quantitative Finance* 12(2): 311–27. DOI:10.1080/14697688.2010.516766.

Bouri, Elie, Rangan Gupta and David Roubaud. 2019. 'Herding Behaviour in Cryptocurrencies'. *Finance Research Letters* 29(6): 216–21. DOI:10.1016/j.frl.2018.07.008.

Borch, Christian. 2007. 'Crowds and Economic Life: Bringing an Old Figure Back in'. *Economy and Society* 36(4): 549–73. DOI:10.1080/03085140701589448.

———. 2012. *The Politics of Crowds: An Alternative History of Sociology*. Cambridge: Cambridge University Press.

Borch, Christian, and Britta Timm Knudsen. 2013. 'Postmodern Crowds: Re-inventing Crowd Thinking'. *Distinkton: Journal of Social Theory* 14(2): 109–13. DOI:10.1080/1600910X.2013.821012.

Borge-Holthoefer, Javier, Sandra González-Bailón, Alejandro Rivero and Yamir Moreno. 2014. 'The Spanish "Indignados" Movement: Time Dynamics, Geographical Distribution, and Recruitment Mechanisms', in Nitin Agarwal, Merlyna Lim and Rolf T. Wigand (eds), *Online Collective Action: Dynamics of the Crowd in Social Media*. Vienna: Springer, pp. 155–77.

Burrell, Jenna. 2009. 'The Field Site as a Network: A Strategy for Locating Ethnographic Research'. *Field Methods* 21(2): 181–99. DOI:10.1177/1525822X08329699.

Canetti, Elias. 1962. *Crowds and Power*, Carol Stewart (trans.). New York: Viking Press.

Clough, Patricia T. 2008. 'Introduction', in Patricia T. Clough and Jean Halley (eds), *The Affective Turn: Theorizing the Social*. Durham, NC: Duke University Press, pp. 1–33.

CoinMarketCap. 2023. 'Cryptocurrency Prices, Charts and Market Capitalizations'. Retrieved 31 March 2023 from https://coinmarketcap.com.

Coleman, Rebecca. 2018. 'Social Media and the Materialisation of the Affective Present', in Tony Sampson, Stephen Maddison and Darren Ellis (eds), *Affect and Social Media: Emotion, Mediation,*

Anxiety and Contagion. London: Rowman & Littlefield, pp. 67–142.
Cova, Bernard. 1997. 'Community and Consumption: Towards a Definition of the "Linking Value" of Product or Services'. *European Journal of Marketing* 31(3): 297–316. DOI:10.1108/03090569710162380.
De Goede, Marieke. 2005. *Virtue, Fortune, and Faith: A Genealogy of Finance*. Minneapolis: University of Minnesota Press.
Dodd, Nigel. 2018. 'The Social Life of Bitcoin'. *Theory, Culture & Society* 35(3): 35–56. DOI:10.1177/0263276417746464.
Durkheim, Emile. 1995 [1912]. *The Elementary Forms of Religious Life*, Karen E. Fields (trans.). New York: The Free Press.
Falzon, Mark-Anthony. 2009. *Multi-Sited Ethnography Theory, Praxis and Locality in Contemporary Research*. Abingdon: Routledge.
Faria, Inês. 2022. 'When Tales of Money Fail: The Importance of Price, Trust and Sociality for Cryptocurrency Users'. *Journal of Cultural Economy* 15(1): 81–92. DOI:10.1080/17530350.2021.1974070.
GWI. 2022. 'Connecting the Dots: Consumer Trends to Know in 2022'. https://www.gwi.com/reports/connecting-the-dots-2022.
Hassoun, Jean-Pierre. 2005. 'Emotions on the Trading Floor: Social and Symbolic Expressions', in Karen Knorr Cetina and Alex Preda (eds), *The Sociology of Financial Markets*. Oxford: Oxford University Press, pp. 102–20.
Hayden, Cori. 2021. 'From Connection to Contagion'. *Journal of the Royal Anthropological Institute* 27(S1): 95–107. DOI:10.1111/1467-9655.13482.
Huh, Eun Young, Joachim Vosgerau and Carey K. Morewedge. 2014. 'Social Defaults: Observed Choices Become Choice Defaults'. *Journal of Consumer Research* 41(3): 746–60. DOI:10.1086/677315.
Kamath, Y. Krishna and James Caverlee. 2011. 'Transient Crowd Discovery on the Real-Time Social Web'. *International Conference on Web Search and Data Mining (WSDM 2011)*, Hong Kong, 9–12 February. DOI:10.1145/1935826.1935909.
Keipi, Teo and Atte Oksanen. 2012. 'Youth Online: Anonymity, Peer Interaction and Linked Subjectivity in Social Media'. Paper presented at *To Be Young! Youth and the Future*, Turku, Finland, 6–8 June, pp. 16–27.
King, Timothy and Dimitrios Koutmos. 2021. 'Herding and Feedback Trading in Cryptocurrency Markets'. *Annals of Operations Research* 300(1): 79–96. DOI:10.1007/s10479-020-03874-4.

Kozinets, V. Robert. 2010. *Netnography: Doing Ethnographic Research Online*. London: Sage.

———. 2015. *Netnography: Redefined*, 2nd edn. Los Angeles: Sage.

Le Bon, Gustave. (1896) 2001. *The Crowd: A Study of the Popular Mind*. Kitchener: Batoche.

Lee, Seung Cheol. 2020. 'Magical Capitalism, Gambler Subjects: South Korea's Bitcoin Investment Frenzy'. *Cultural Studies* 36(1): 96–119. DOI:10.1080/09502386.2020.1788620.

Lünenborg, Margreth. 2020. 'Affective Publics: Understanding the Dynamic Formation of Public Articulations beyond the Public Sphere', in Anne Fleig and Christian von Scheve (eds), *Public Spheres of Resonance: Constellations of Affect and Language*. Abingdon: Routledge, pp. 30–48.

Marcus, E. George. 1995. 'Ethnography in/of the World System: The Emergence of Multi-sited Ethnography'. *Annual Review of Anthropology* 24(1): 95–117. DOI:10.1146/annurev.an.24.100195.000523.

Maurer, Bill, Taylor C. Nelms and Lana Swartz. 2013. '"When Perhaps the Real Problem is Money Itself!": The Practical Materiality of Bitcoin'. *Social Semiotics* 23(2): 261–77. DOI:10.1080/10350330.2013.777594.

Morais, M. Greiciele, Valdeci F. Santos and Carlos A. Gonçalves. 2020. 'Netnography: Origins, Foundations, Evolution and Axiological and Methodological Developments and Trends'. *The Qualitative Report* 25(2): 441–55.

Murphy, J. John. 1999. *Technical Analysis of the Financial Markets: A Comprehensive Guide to Trading Methods and Applications*. Paramus: New York Institute of Finance.

Nakamoto, Satoshi. 2008. 'Bitcoin: A Peer-to-Peer Electronic Cash System'. Retrieved 7 March 2023 from https://bitcoin.org/bitcoin.pdf.

Nelms, C. Taylor, Bill Maurer, Lana Swartz and Scott Mainwaring. 2018. 'Social Payments: Innovation, Trust, Bitcoin, and the Sharing Economy'. *Theory, Culture & Society* 35(3): 13–33. DOI:10.1177/0263276417746466.

Orléan, André. 2014. *The Empire of Value: A New Foundation for Economics*. Cambridge, MA: MIT Press.

Philippas, Dionisis, Nikolaos Philippas, Panagiotis Tziogkidis and Hatem Rjiba. 2020. 'Signal-Herding in Cryptocurrencies'. *Journal of International Financial Markets, Institutions and Money* 65(3): 101191. DOI:10.1016/j.intfin.2020.101191.

Pink, Sarah, Heather Horst, John Postill, Larissa Hjorth, Tanja Lewis, Jo Tacchi. 2016. *Digital Ethnography: Principals and Practices*. Los Angeles: Sage.

Poyser, Obryan. 2018. 'Herding Behavior in Cryptocurrency Markets'. Paper 1806.11348v2, arXiv.org. DOI:10.48550/arXiv.1806.11348.

Reicher, Stephen. 2004. 'The Psychology of Crowd Dynamics', in Michael A. Hogg and R. Scott Tindale (eds), *Blackwell Handbook of Social Psychology: Group Processes*. Hoboken, NJ: John Wiley & Sons, pp. 182–208.

Ringrose, Jessica and Kaitlynn Mendes. 2018. 'Mediated Affect and Feminist Solidarity Teens Using Twitter to Challenge "Rape Culture" in and around School', in Tony Sampson, Stephen Maddison and Darren Ellis (eds), *Affect and Social Media: Emotion, Mediation, Anxiety and Contagion*. London: Rowman & Littlefield, pp. 85–98.

Röggla, Kathrin. 2019. 'It's the Language, Stupid', in Anne Fleig and Christian von Scheve (eds), *Public Spheres of Resonance: Constellations of Affect and Language*. Abingdon: Routledge, pp. 17–28.

Sampson, Tony. 2012. *Virality: Contagion Theory in the Age of Networks*. Minneapolis: University of Minnesota Press.

Sampson, Tony, Stephen Maddison and Darren Ellis (eds). 2018. *Affect and Social Media: Emotion, Mediation, Anxiety and Contagion*. London: Rowman & Littlefield.

Schroeder, Rob, Sean F. Everton, Russel Shepherd. 2014. 'The Strength of Tweet Ties', in Nitin Agarwal, Merlyna Lim and Rolf T. Wigand (eds), *Online Collective Action: Dynamics of the Crowd in Social Media*. Vienna: Springer, pp. 179–192.

Snodgrass, G. Jeffrey. 2014. 'Ethnography of Online Cultures', in H. Russel Bernard and Clarence C. Gravlee (eds), *Handbook of Methods in Cultural Anthropology*. Lanham, MD: Rowman & Littlefield, pp. 465–95.

Stage, Carsten. 2013. 'The Online Crowd: A Contradiction in Terms? On the Potentials of Gustave Le Bon's Crowd Psychology in an Analysis of Affective Blogging'. *Distinktion: Journal of Social Theory* 14(2): 211–26. DOI:10.1080/1600910X.2013.773261.

Stäheli, Urs. 2006. 'Market Crowds', in Jeffrey T Schnapps and Matthew Tiews (eds), *Crowds*. Stanford: Stanford University Press, pp. 271–77.

Syndicus, Ivo. 2018. 'Crowds, Affect, and the Mediation of Emergent Collectivities: A Student Strike in Papua New Guinea as an

Order-Making Project'. *Anthropological Forum* 28(4): 377–93. DOI:10.1080/00664677.2018.1541785.

Tan, Lin, Thomas C. Chiang, Joseph R. Mason and Edward Nelling. 2008. 'Herding Behavior in Chinese Stock Markets: An Examination of A and B Shares'. *Pacific-Basin Finance Journal* 16(1–2): 61–77. DOI:10.1016/j.pacfin.2007.04.004.

Tarde, Gabriel. 2010 [1969]. *Gabriel Tarde: On Communication and Social Influence*, Terry N. Clark (ed.). Chicago: University of Chicago Press.

Tardi, Carla. 2021. 'Genesis Block: Bitcoin Definition, Mysteries, Secret Message'. *Investopedia*. Retrieved 19 August 2023 from https://www.investopedia.com/terms/g/genesis-block.asp.

Tutenges, Sébastien. 2015. 'Pub Crawls at a Bulgarian Nightlife Resort: A Case Study Using Crowd Theory'. *Tourist Studies* 15(3): 283–99. DOI:10.1177/1468797615597856.

Vennonen, Anna. 2023. 'More Than Money: An Ethnography of Dreams, Value and Community in the Cryptoscene', MA thesis. Helsinki: University of Helsinki.

Warner, Michael. 2002. 'Publics and Counterpublics'. *Public Culture* 14(1): 49–90. DOI:10.1215/08992363-14-1-49.

UNSTRUCTURED SIMPLICITY
The Peer-to-Peer Collective and Concurrent Formations of Cryptocommunities

Mitchell Tuddenham

Introduction

Prior to the early 2000s, the most common computing model was the client/server model. Simply put, the client/server model is where 'an application residing on a client computer invokes commands at a server' (Singh 2001: 4), revealing a dyadic relational, or hierarchical, structure throughout its network. The server plays host to the client's commands, setting up two distinct operations. On the one hand, the client demands a certain response from the server. On the other hand, the server is necessary, even vital, for the client's functionality. A common problem for this type of computing model is that the centralization of information 'makes for performance bottlenecks and for overall system susceptibility to single-point failure' (Singh 2001: 4). For cyberattacks to be successful, all that needs to be targeted is the centralized server. If the server fails, this affects each clients' ability to operate. Hence, power over the flow of information rests with the centralized server. Moreover, the client/server model is inefficient when it comes to information processing, bandwidth and computing resources. With the amount of information on the internet constantly increasing, single search engines and data centres cannot locate and catalogue the information efficiently. Additionally, whilst new fibre cables are installed and provide additional bandwidth, 'hot spots just get hotter and cold pipes remain unused' (Gong 2002: 37).

Immense pressure is put on space and power consumption (Gong 2002). With the generation of new developments in computing, there needed to be a better way to organize the efficiency of the relied-upon computing model. Moreover, the client/server model's faults needed to be mitigated to account for improvements in cyberattack methods and in response to growing concerns around centralized control (Hughes 1993). Thus, to better utilize internet and computing resources, a more distributed type of computing model was introduced, namely that of a *peer-to-peer* computing network.

Peer-to-peer (P2P) networks are commonly associated with file-sharing programs, such as Napster, which enabled the sharing of mp3 compressed audio files (Schollmeier 2001). In its most basic form, a P2P network is where two or more devices are linked to each other 'without requiring a separate server computer or server software' (Cope 2002). Schollmeier (2001) defines P2P networks based on what he calls a *servent*, which is derived from the first syllable of the term 'server' and the second syllable of the term 'client'. Hence, for Schollmeier (2001), the term *servent* represents the capability of the nodes within a P2P network to simultaneously act as both client and server. This ability means that the network's space and power consumption, in terms of information processing and storage, bandwidth, and computing resources, is distributed throughout the network and thus better utilized.

As a more efficient way of organizing network operations, P2P structures have a direct impact on power dynamics and hierarchical relations. This is what concerns the present discussion. The offered material derives mostly from research that amounted to approximately ten months of observation of online forums and other accessible resources from the public domain. Rather than conducting what can be described as a 'traditional' ethnography involving long-term exposure to 'real-life' people and events, I instead focused on the presence of the cryptocurrency emergence within middle-class circles across the world that supersede the Global North/South divisions and aimed to gain a critical understanding of the mechanics of the blockchain. Thus, this chapter methodologically concentrates on the broader Bitcoin/crypto philosophy and the mechanical and practical structures that underpin it. Out of this, I broadly aim to elaborate on what cryptocurrency and its associated ideals can do for our understanding of human beings and the way we organize ourselves within the context of a changing world order – in this case, with a particular focus on the tensions between crypto crowds and coin communities.

More specifically, this chapter aims, first, to further the critical idea of 'blockchain dehierarchicalization'[1] (Berg et al. 2019) by developing an understanding of the blockchain network in terms of *transindividuation*. Second, it aims to utilize this understanding as a means to explore and articulate the tensions between the crypto crowd (expressed as the P2P network) and concentrated cryptocommunities. Through a critical analysis of the original Bitcoin white paper and an example of a practical blockchain transaction, I aim to address the idea that the blockchain 'flattens' hierarchy and introduces a kind of horizontality to market and social relations. This will lead to the question of 'what reconceptions of market and social organization does the blockchain reveal?'. It is at this point that *transindividuation* will be introduced to extend the idea of 'dehierarchicalization' and cover any gaps that horizontality may leave.

For Simondon (via Combes 2012) and Stiegler (Stiegler and Rogoff 2010), 'transindividuation' is the co-construction of the individual and the collective through one another. The blockchain, through its purported mechanistic decentralization and P2P network dynamics, initiates a construction of human–human relations between crypto supporters that go beyond an existing spatial and temporal understanding. Out of this, a call to rethink conceptions of blockchain crowd formations can be made. In addition, this particular form of collective dynamics can be linked back to the developing utopian ideal and also conflated in the organization of (typically offline) communities and events, such as 'Bitcoin Halving Day' and the annual Bitcoin Conference. This connection between blockchain utopian ideals, the P2P dynamic and the forming of communities expresses a certain idea of crowd-community production dynamics, of which the understanding can be enhanced, I suggest, via the concept of *transindividuation*.

P2P Horizontality: Structure and Practice

P2P computing alters the dynamic of the client/server model to distribute power throughout the network. In the same article cited earlier, Gong (2002: 37) writes that P2P computing models 'adopt a network-based computing style that neither excludes nor inherently depends on centralized control points'. This style of computing generates a more heterogenous dynamic and a distribution of power relations between nodes. It is this decentralization and distribution of computing power that led to Satoshi Nakamoto, the founder of Bitcoin, adopting the P2P model for the structure of Bitcoin's operating mechanism, the blockchain (Nakamoto 2008). The Bitcoin network uses cryptography and network computing to accomplish what has traditionally been achieved by third parties. Transaction data and blocks do not pass through any central authority; instead, consensus is determined by the entire network, as every working node validates a block (and its transaction data) by using that block's hash to find the next block in the sequence. The longest chain of sequential blocks is taken as the correct chain as it possesses the 'greatest proof-of-work effort invested in it' (ibid.: 3), representing the majority decision.

Paired with new encryption methods arising from developments in cryptography, this particular structuring of the blockchain forms the basis for the promotion of initial cryptocurrencies as 'horizontal markets' (Bousfield 2019). The cryptoanarchist and cypherpunk visions underpinning Bitcoin's emergence were both founded on a strong distrust for centralized governance, particularly of financial markets (Hughes 1993; May 1988). Today, these visions are still very much alive, with many crypto enthusiasts believing in utopian ideals that render the blockchain as the disruptive technology that will 'create a society with horizontal structures and distributed authority' (Atzori 2017: 27).

Some are calling the horizontality of the blockchain's governing and organizing dynamic a 'dehierarchicalization' (Berg et al. 2019). The idea of a dehierarchicalized 'horizontal' structure of social and political order implies the conception of ordinary (nonblockchain) society in terms of verticality. In other words, the power relations and governing dynamics of nonblockchain hierarchical structures are seen as a top-down organization of society. The idea is that the blockchain flattens this hierarchical verticality to create a more heterogeneous social organization. There are two components to this: horizontality happens (1) via the network's structure (the blockchain's operation), and

(2) in practice (how users interact with blockchain). First, what exactly within the blockchain's structure entertains the utopian vision of horizontally distributed authority and a heterogeneous society? Let us turn to the Bitcoin white paper and Nakamoto's own description of the blockchain network to answer these questions.

Blocks are made up of cryptographically encoded transaction data. The cryptography used to encode the transaction of coins from one party to another essentially allows the receiving party to validate the originality of the coin (see Nakamoto 2008: 2). However, there remains the need to check for what Nakamoto (2008) calls the 'double spend problem' – there needs to be a way to check that the previous owner of the coin did not duplicate it. Traditionally, this is done by the mint or the bank, meaning that a third-party intermediary would hold the power to process transactions. To displace this location of power, Nakamoto turned to a P2P network structure based on the proof-of-work cryptography mechanism, whereby transaction inputs are at once private and secure whilst also being public and transparent.

Nakamoto (2008: 8) describes the blockchain's security as deriving from the network's 'unstructured simplicity'. Loosely, 'unstructured simplicity' refers to the P2P network and proof-of-work mechanism. The unstructured simplicity of the network is as follows: nodes work simultaneously, all at once, with little coordination. New transactions are broadcast to all nodes, whilst each node collates them into a block. When a node successfully finds the right proof-of-work for its block – that is, when it finds a nonce value that satisfies the target value – it broadcasts that block directly to the rest of the network. Other nodes express confirmation and acceptance by using that block to find the proof-of-work for the next block. Hence, the proof-of-work mechanism takes the place that is traditionally held by third parties. New nodes can join the network at any time while other nodes leave. They can even leave and rejoin, taking the proof-of-work of the chain as proof of what happened whilst they were offline (Nakamoto 2008). The network structure is thus a fluid, dynamic and constant redisbursement of power relations. Moreover, the network exists in a dynamic of potential. The map of power never looks the same, but the same result is always achieved: a nonce is found and a block is broadcast to the network. The node that finds the nonce and broadcasts the block is almost always never the same as the previous block.

Geospatially, the blockchain imagines a world without national and state borders, compass points and datelines. The blockchain encompasses the globe; the P2P network operates transnationally, transitioning the globe into the digital realm. By virtue of the P2P set-up, for example, physical store vendors on the beaches in Costa Rica (Grudgings 2022) are part of a network that spans the globe, connecting with both large industrial Bitcoin mining rigs in Iceland (Mallonee 2019) and smaller 'wildcat' Bitcoin miners in homes and offices (DuPont 2019; Zimmer 2017). Whilst the geospatial conditions that confronted many groups of humans in the past are now conjoined with the digital, the blockchain is the ordering principle that provides a geometry for the operation of transactions, exchange and relations in cyberspace. Larger-scale computer nodes co-construct the network with smaller 'wildcat' miners. It is a global imagination, navigating the contours of cyberspace with a logic that organizes, orients and directs. In other words, it instils an idealistic and utopian geospatial planetary and social order – one without the existence of borders, the limiting properties of distance and the dominating effects of hegemony.

Let us look at an example of a transaction in practice. The first known transaction of Bitcoins for 'real-world' goods took place on 22 May 2010, when Laszlo Hanyecz traded 10,000 Bitcoins for two large pizzas (George 2022). Initially, Hanyecz posted to a forum, writing: 'I'll pay 10,000 bitcoins for a couple of pizzas' (Laszlo 2010). Soon after, a student by the name of Jeremy Sturdivant took him up on his offer. Sturdivant purchased the pizzas from Papa Johns and delivered them to Hanyecz, for which he was transferred 10,000 Bitcoins for his services. To transfer the Bitcoins, Hanyecz used Sturdivant's wallet address to input the transaction to the Bitcoin program that broadcast it to all other nodes. The operation of the P2P blockchain took care of the rest. 'I just want to report that I successfully traded 10,000 bitcoins for pizza' remarked Hanyecz in a follow-up forum post (Laszlo 2010). Resulting from the utilization of the blockchain and its P2P structure, the interaction and resulting transaction between Hanyecz and Sturdivant was direct, personal and secure. Thus, this process differs significantly from 'traditional' modes of exchange. Moreover, so do the kinds of ontological positions and relational interactions between humans that this process engenders, as is evident in the Bitcoin-for-pizza transaction.

Relations in the 'traditional' financial system are typically defined relative to the centre (banks, the mint, the state, etc. are seen as centralized points of control). As the locus of power, with the capacity to affect, direct, inhibit, restrict and delay, these intermediaries construct an apparatus of determination. Financial exchange of this nature, always watched over by the eye of Big Brother, limits the contingencies and potency of human individuals in their capacity to affect one another. In contrast, the blockchain heuristically disrupts the status quo that conventional systems have imposed upon the world. It embraces an open character, altering the point of exchange and the forces in relations.

The centre/periphery, internal/external relations (recall the client/server model) are no longer useful or applicable when there is no single centre of power, as is the case with the blockchain. Rather, there is a multiplicity of 'centres' (i.e. locations) that exist in the network, making it difficult to define ontosocial positions without an anchor to a sole centre point. This means that, ontologically speaking, the P2P network places the one in relation to the many rather than in relation to the mass (that is, the mass of power). In the case of Laszlo Hanyecz and Jeremy Sturdivant's Bitcoin-for-pizza exchange, the transaction was made without corresponding with centralized points of control. Rather, Hanyecz let the proof-of-work mechanism verify his coins and the transaction of these coins. Both Hanyecz and Sturdivant were subjecting themselves in relation to the many nodes across the network and the corresponding proof-of work cycle, as opposed to the mass of power that a third-party intermediary would hold. They were also placing themselves in a more direct relation to each other.

Problematizing Conceptions of Blockchain Hierarchy

Here, I wish to problematize the idea of horizontality, but also to expand on the idea of 'dehierarchicalization' put forward by Berg et al. (2019). Although horizontality captures something of the blockchain's effects on organizational structures, in my estimations this conceptual understanding can be extended upon to further encapsulate a more accurate depiction of the blockchain's hierarchical conceptions. Using a vertical/horizontal axis to describe the blockchain network's hierarchy is problematic for multiple reasons.

First, the network's arrangement is not two-dimensional. Conceptually, the vertical/horizontal axis on which hierarchy is often measured is a two-dimensional scale. In a two-dimensional scale, removing (or 'flattening') the traditional hierarchy of verticality and concentrated control points (i.e. the client/server computing model) would indeed shift the arrangement into what would seem a more horizontal structure. However, the blockchain network is a three-dimensional structure without a top/bottom scale, derived from the fact that the network is arranged relative to *multiple* places of convergent forces – that is, 'centres' of power – as opposed to one centre and its periphery. The totality of the P2P network paradoxically[2] works together to achieve consensus. Again, this demonstrates the absence of a top/bottom scale. Hence, the hierarchy of the blockchain network – its 'sacred order' – evokes a sense of Dumont's (1980) 'encompassing relations' in that each node – each position in the network – has its own role in actualizing potential. Thus, whilst it acknowledges the blockchain network's 'flattening' of vertical hierarchy, thinking of the network in terms of a two-dimensional arrangement does not capture the whole picture. Instead, a consideration of its three-dimensionality would encapsulate the horizontality, but also account for a more holistic understanding of the blockchain network.

Second, the network is not closed and static. Using the vertical/horizontal axis to describe the hierarchical order of the blockchain implies that the order is set, static and unchanging. However, that is clearly not the case with the blockchain network; instead, its 'unstructured simplicity' (its dynamic potential) means that it is an *open* system of dynamic relations. As new nodes come online and as other nodes go offline, as the value of Bitcoin booms and busts, and as the reward for mining decreases, the locations of power move and morph throughout the network. There are no predefined roles that imply a status of power as there are with the client/server computing model. Yet, whilst the network itself is constantly shifting and morphing, in practice – for instance, the Bitcoin-for-pizza transaction – the relations between the two transacting parties stay constant and consistent until the exchange is complete, adding another level of complexity that the vertical/horizontal scale does not cover. Analytically, I interpret this dynamism and network fluidity as a totalization of relations – an encompassment of the whole network. Thus, hierarchical conceptions of the blockchain, again, should be closer to those of Dumont (1980) than to that of a reliance on a vertical/horizontal axis.

From this, we can suggest that thinking in terms of horizontal/vertical conceptions to determine the hierarchical structure of the network does not capture the dynamic of the P2P network and the dimensionality of its arrangement, nor does it capture the positionality in which its users find themselves (i.e. the positionality of Hanyecz and Sturdivant in their Bitcoin-for-pizza exchange). Thus, the arrangement of multiple power locations and the dynamic potential of the network's structure requires a reconceptualization of hierarchy. Moreover, the total redisbursement of concentrations of power contributes to the value of trustlessness that is foundational to Bitcoin's network operations, adding yet another layer of complexity that calls for a consideration of the way we conceptualize the blockchain collective arrangement.

Blockchain, computing and cryptography enthusiasts desire the automation of trust (May 1988). The structure of the network as a P2P model renders third-party intermediaries in the act of exchange as obsolete[3] and relies on network consensus to carry out the tasks usually completed by these intermediaries. 'We have proposed a system for electronic transactions without relying on trust' declared Satoshi Nakamoto (2008: 8). Trust in social relations[4] is eliminated and replaced by cryptography and the realm of the machinic. Such social interactions are frictionless, in the sense that no third-party acts as a guardian for successful transactions. The machinic repetition of the blockchain's proof-of-work cycle breaks down existing notions of trust via the essential step of attaining network consensus. In the case of decentralized cryptocurrency systems, such as the Bitcoin system, it is the P2P network itself that facilitates and regulates exchanges, checking for double-spending and validating transactions and coins, meaning that the whole of the wider network is incorporated into every transaction.

This fact gives us the possibility to consider the concept of transindividuation in articulating the network's dynamic of crowd production and modulation. In other words, we are presented with a possibility to consider what 'dehierarchicalization' might look like. Transindividuation, developed by Bernard Stiegler (Stiegler and Rogoff 2010; Stiegler et al. 2012) and Simondon (via Combes 2012), helps to reconceptualize the blockchain's hierarchical collective by virtue of the network's P2P co-construction of the one and the many. To put it another way, the network's individual nodes work together as a totality to achieve consensus in the facilitation of transactions and to keep relations between users direct and secure, which can be expressed, I suggest, as a process of transindividuation. It is through this concept that I will comment on the crowding and collective dynamics that are associated with blockchain technology and the wider crypto sphere.

P2P Transindividuation

To expand on the idea of a 'dehierarchicalization' that the blockchain network engenders and to conceptualize how this may look, we can turn to the crowd theory concept of *transindividuation*. Consider the geospatiality of the blockchain network. Through the distribution and decentralization of power relations across the encompassed globe (for example, from Costa Rica to Iceland), the potential of the whole system – that of the collective (or the crowd) – is realized/actualized by the whole system itself. This is in contrast with a centralized system, the trajectory of which is mediated by a centralized single entity. For the blockchain, the direction of the system – or the movement of potential to actual – is rather influenced by the whole collective as a relatively free-flowing and generally open crowd of network peers. Recalling my earlier statement, it is the many as opposed to the mass (of power) that directs the movement of potential to actual. The actualization of the state of the network is directly informed by the fact of the network's decentralized and 'dehierarchialized' nature. Here is where, I suggest, *transindividuation* comes in.[5] This accumulative force of the whole network – the collective (crowds and communities included) – that happens through decentralization is the key to this idea.

For Simondon, being part of a group is not defined by a 'sociological belonging', but instead 'comes into existence when the forces of the future harboured within a number of living individuals lead to a collective structuration' (Combes 2012: 43). A collective does not involve a mere assemblage of individuals, but rather a 'movement of self-constitution' (ibid.). Similarly, for Stiegler, 'the concept of "transindividuation" is one that does not rest with the individuated "I" or with the interindividuated "We", but is the process of co-individuation … in which both the "I" and the "We" are transformed through one another' (2010: paragraph 3). It is this transformation of the singular through the multiple, and vice versa, that constitutes the process of transindividuation.

Aligning with Rantala (2019), I envision the blockchain as a medium for transindividuation: the latter is achieved by the former's capacity for decentralization and distribution. In other words, the network's unstructured simplicity engenders the transindividuation process. Rantala (ibid.: 1) describes the transindividual relation as the 'possibility of a concurrent problem-solving at the collective and individual level'. In the case of the blockchain, it is quite literally a concurrent problem solving, with each peer aiming to solve the cryptographic problem of finding the satisfactory nonce value. Only one peer can 'win', but it is the network's collective force that moves the blockchain forward. Hence, the blockchain collective is constructed via the accumulative force harboured by 'peers'. But the blockchain's social network is not an assemblage of already-individuated 'peers'; rather, the singular 'peer' and the multiple 'peer(s)' are transformed through one another in a movement of collective self-constitution – i.e. 'P2P'. As they race against each other to find the nonce – that is, as they participate in the process of differentiating themselves from each other – network peers are simultaneously co-constructing the network and aligning themselves with other peers to form a totality. It is an accumulation of the force of the collective network to determine the state of the blockchain (which can be taken as the state of the world) and the crowds and communities, as part of this collective, make up this accumulative force.

Desired futures and utopian visions converge on one another to form the accumulative force of the P2P blockchain collective in actualizing potential. The one and the many co-construct each other. If the network was centralized, it would not differentiate the individuals and thus would not provide a 'frame of pre-individual potentiality' (Rantala 2019: 13). The peer is individuated in the process of the blockchain's proof-of-work mechanism; individuation occurs within the process of being differentiated from other peers, but is simultaneously collectivized within the network's accumulative power. Here, the process leads to the concurrent realization of the potentials of both individuals and the collective (see Combes 2012). This form of transindividuation, derived from the decentralized P2P network, engenders a particular mode of crowd dynamics – the accumulation of collective forces that could not be achieved without the sense of transindividuality harboured by decentralization. In other words, as Rantala (2019: 13, emphasis in original) writes, 'blockchain can be seen as *a crystallisation of the power to create methods and processes of decentralised organisation,* which can lead to further individuations by individuals themselves'.

Transindividuation helps to reconceptualize blockchain hierarchies by virtue of the network's co-construction of the one and the many. It captures the blockchain's P2P dynamism and fluidity, as the network nodes co-create both themselves (as nodes) and the blockchain as a total network. In other words, the singular and the multiple co-construct each other, as all nodes work concurrently and paradoxically; each node races all other nodes to secure the next sequential block, but they also work in unison to develop the network and achieve the aim of decentralization. The actualizing of a potential blockchain arrangement at any given point in time is determined by the co-construction of individual nodes acting paradoxically in simultaneous competition and collective unison. Moreover, transacting parties (such as Hanyecz and Sturdivant) are also bonded to each other by this co-constructing process of network transindividuation. In the context of the blockchain as a practical P2P network, transindividuation extends the idea of 'dehierarchicalization' and helps us to understand how it is achieved.

Furthermore, because of its contribution to hierarchical reconceptions, blockchain transindividuation is connected to the formation of blockchain (and other cryptography-related) communities that converge around the potentiality of utopian – 'dehierarchicalized' – worlds. As a more encompassing depiction of total network organization, transindividuation encapsulates this expressed blockchain utopia. In other words, the blockchain network, by virtue of the collective's accumulative forces in actualizing potential – the network's process of transindividuation – drives the generation of the blockchain utopian ideal.

Concurrent Formations of Cryptocommunities

We can determine that the P2P blockchain collective can best be thought of as being a process of transindividuation rather than relying on a vertical/horizontal axis to describe the network's hierarchical effects. To conclude, I wish to complete the analysis by holding this particular expression of P2P network dynamics up to the formation of cryptocommunities and events as a way of encouraging further points of discussion. In other words, I wish to comment on the P2P collective's association, as a process of transindividuation, to smaller community phenomena in the crypto space.

In the present analysis, the crowd has been interpreted as the P2P blockchain network, operating as an open, self-regulating (or self-referential) dynamic phenomenon (see Canetti 1984 [1960]), as it continues to expand, contract, shift and morph through both cyberspace and geospace. Contrarily, smaller, more rigid cryptocommunities are typically less fluid in their formation, organization and development, often occurring blockchain-adjacent in other online spaces (such as Reddit) or perhaps with a hybrid geocyberspace presence (as did the *Bitcoin 2022* conference, happening simultaneously in Miami, Florida, and on YouTube). However, they are typically convergent on utopian ideals of decentralization and trustlessness (see Faustino et al. 2021; Swartz 2018). Hence, their formation is driven, at least partly, by the transindividuation of blockchain peers. In other words, as a process of transindividuation and dehierarchicalization, the P2P network is a modality for the advancement of utopian visions.[6] Here, the tension between the encompassing crypto crowds and localized cryptocommunities manifests as a bridge between the two existences, as the philosophy derived from the dynamics of the crypto crowd (the transindividualized P2P network) is the driving force that generates the perpetuation of (some) popular cryptocommunities. It is hoped that this conclusion ties the present chapter closer to this volume's wider topic.

I have already mentioned Laszlo Hanyecz's purchase of pizza on 22 May 2010. This date is now annually celebrated as 'Bitcoin Pizza Day' in commemoration of the first known 'real-world' transaction using Bitcoins. 'Bitcoin Pizza Day' celebrates the utopian aim of a world predicated on trustlessness – that is, a world predicated on P2P dynamics. The celebration of 'Bitcoin Pizza Day' marks the breaking down of existing formations and the remaking of new potentialities made possible by the dynamics of P2P networks. In some ways, it is a reaffirmation of the utopian ideals that are predicated on the decentralized nature of the blockchain's P2P network. Moreover, it is a kind of mythification of the aspirations of a new sociality. As Faustino et al. (2021: 74) state, 'cyclical celebrations . . . perform an important role in retaining collective memory about [the blockchain's] achievements'. In addition, there are other examples that carry out a similar process.

For instance, 'Bitcoin Halving Day' is another cyclical commemoration, this time marking the point when the mining reward for the Bitcoin network halves in value.[7] This event happens roughly every four years (or, more precisely, every 210,000 blocks) and is met by the cryptocommunity with a 'festive spirit' (Faustino et al. 2021: 74). Communities form around various webpages and online forums to celebrate the occasion. For the halving that occurred on 12 May 2020, websites hosted live countdowns to the Halving and wished users a 'Happy Bitcoin Halving #3' (Faustino et al. 2021). Again, this celebration is predicated upon a fundamental aspect of the blockchain's decentralizing operation – the halving of the proof-of-work reward – thereby conflating the formation of communities with the utopian thinking emerging out of the P2P network.

Finally, annual or periodic conferences held online and in the 'real' world, such as *Bitcoin 2022*, are another example of the conflation of blockchain collective dynamics in driving localized communities. At *Bitcoin 2022*, the 'most important aspects' of Bitcoin were celebrated, including decentralization and freedom, with the main focus being 'unlocking human potential' (Russell 2022). Discussions at these conferences and smaller blockchain meet-ups typically focus on the 'good' of the blockchain (Russell 2022) – that is, its usefulness in achieving utopian visions of decentralized social, political and economic organization. At *Bitcoin 2022*, presentations about grand visions of utopian society were followed by lectures on the latest technological developments to blockchain technology and vice versa. The idealistic is merged with the technical at these community meet-ups to substantialize the crowd dynamics of the 'unstructured' P2P network. Thus, it is the fundamentality of the Bitcoin blockchain as a P2P network, demonstrated in Nakamoto's Bitcoin white paper of 2008, and the concurrent processes of transindividuation that I am connecting to the formation of convergent communities and associated events.

The convergent forming of cryptocommunities around events that progress the mythification of the blockchain utopia evoke a sense of concurrent 'flows of desire' (Combes 2012: 52) – a coming together to realize collective imaginaries. Almost a kind of extension of network transindividuation, the dehierarchicalization of the P2P network – its 'unstructured simplicity' (Nakamoto 2008: 8) – is conflated in the cryptocommunities that emerge out of celebrations surrounding decentralization. However, tensions between crypto crowds and communities arise here – on the one hand, a generalizing and open dynamic (the crowd), and on the other hand, a dynamic that is less fluid (the community) – as the two apparently opposing dynamics demonstrate their connections.

Lana Swartz (2021) says it best: 'Today's cryptocurrency communities are . . . summoning a future.' The futures that many of these localized cryptocommunity formations aim to construct are premised on utopian ideals drawn out of the fundamentals of the transindividuating machine that is the blockchain. In other words, the formation of localized communities carefully constructs collective visions based on loose structuration, trustlessness and subjugation by external (technologic and cryptographic) means, all of which extend from the transindividuated crowd dynamics. Thus, in closing, I wish to highlight an idea alluded to by Matan Shapiro in the Introduction to the present volume and an idea that I believe is central to what has been presented here: the cyclicity of the singular and the multiple or of crowd and community dynamics. In other words, individuals harness the power of the crowd to form communities. These communities in turn enforce the crowd in a cyclical rather than dialectical or antagonistic fashion. Hence, conflated in the localized (offline) communities and the mythification of the blockchain utopia is the accumulation of collective forces in P2P blockchain networks, insofar as the P2P arrangement offers us an opportunity to articulate a framework for understanding the network's collective organization in the context of the blockchain utopia. The convergent communities anchor themselves to the utopian visions that can be drawn out of the blockchain collective dynamics predicated on transindividuation, that is, on a reconceptualization of collective organization.

Acknowledgements

I wish to thank Gillian Tan for her generosity in providing insightful comments during the writing of this chapter. I also thank Matan Shapiro for the opportunity to be a part of this project and for his efforts in making it all possible.

Mitchell Tuddenham is a sessional tutor at Deakin University, Australia, teaching a class on violence and the state apparatus. His research interests include ritual, cosmology, the Anthropocene, the state and conceptions of violence.

Notes

1. Or, in other words, 'the flattening of hierarchical structures' via the blockchain.
2. It is paradoxical because while all nodes must work together to achieve consensus, each node is racing against all the others to find the target proof-of-work.
3. The encroachment of external centralizations of power is always immanent. For instance, cryptocurrency exchange platforms are highly centralized third parties that do affect network dynamics. However, these external intermediaries rely on the blockchain's P2P operation to function. Hence, these exchange platforms are just one of the many locations of power, adding yet another level of complexity to the crowd and collective dynamics of the blockchain. Furthermore, in the context of crypto crowds and cryptocommunities, these exchange platforms offer yet another instance of community production as they play host to a con-

glomerate of crypto enthusiasts who converge on such platforms to exercise their support for certain cryptocoins.
4. In this case, social relations are represented in the form of cryptographic transactions.
5. Stiegler (2012: 173) even states that digital networks are 'absolutely and radically new' processes of individuation.
6. Such utopian visions are those heralded by the cypherpunks and cryptoanarchists who became a kind of internet community centred around the benefits and importance of cryptography (see May 1988). These groups of people are another example of community production that converges around principles and philosophies expressed by the transindividuating machine, also known as the blockchain network.
7. On 12 May 2020, the reward for mining bitcoins was halved from 12.5 Bitcoins to 6.25 Bitcoins (Faustino et al. 2021).

References

Atzori, Marcella. 2017. 'Blockchain Technology and Decentralised Governance: Is the State Still Necessary?' *Journal of Governance and Regulation* 6(1): 45–62.

Berg, Chris, Sinclair Davidson and Jason Potts. 2020. 'Capitalism after Satoshi: Blockchains, Dehierarchicalisation, Innovation Policy, and the Regulatory State'. *Journal of Entrepreneurship and Public Policy* 9(2): 152–64.

Bousfield, Dan. 2019. 'Crypto-coin Hierarchies: Social Contestation in Blockchain Networks'. *Global Networks* 19(3): 291–307.

Canetti, Elias. 1984 [1960]. *Crowds and Power*. New York: Farrar, Straus & Giroux.

Combes, Muriel. 2012. *Gilbert Simondon and the Philosophy of the Transindividual*, Thomas LaMarre (trans.). Cambridge, MA: MIT Press.

Cope, James. 2002. 'What's a Peer-to-Peer (P2P) Network?' *Computerworld*, 8 April. Retrieved 19 August 2023 from https://www.computerworld.com/article/2588287/networking-peer-to-peer-network.html.

Dumont, Louis. 1980. *Homo Hierarchicus: The Caste System and Its Implications*, Mark Sainsbury, Louis Dumont and Basia Gulati (trans.). Chicago: University of Chicago Press.

DuPont, Quinn. 2019. 'The Financial Frontier Is Hot #BitcoinDynamics'. *Allegra Laboratory*. Retrieved 31 August 2023 from https://allegralaboratory.net/the-financial-frontier-is-hot-bitcoin dynamics/.

Faustino, Sandra, Inês Faria and Rafael Marques. 2021. 'The Myths and Legends of King Satoshi and the Knights of Blockchain'. *Journal of Cultural Economy* 15(1): 67–80.

George, Benedict. 2022. 'What Is Bitcoin Pizza Day?' *CoinDesk*, 7 April. Retrieved 19 August 2023 from https://www.coindesk.com/learn/what-is-bitcoin-pizza-day.

Gong, Li. 2002. 'Guest Editor's Introduction: Peer-to-Peer Networks in Action'. *IEEE Internet Computing* 6(1): 37–39.

Grudgings, Stuart. 2022. 'Bitcoin Beach Spawns a Fast-Growing Offshoot in Costa Rica – Bitcoin Jungle'. *Bitcoin Magazine*, 22 April. Retrieved 19 August 2023 from https://bitcoinmagazine.com/culture/bitcoin-beach-spawns-offshoot.

Hughes, Eric. 1993. 'A Cypherpunk's Manifesto', 9 March. Retrieved 19 August 2023 from https://nakamotoinstitute.org/static/docs/cypherpunk-manifesto.txt.

Laszlo. 2010. 'Pizza for Bitcoins?' *Bitcoin Talk*, 18 May. Retrieved 19 August 2023 from https://bitcointalk.org/index.php?topic=137.0.

Mallonee, Laura. 2019. 'Inside the Icelandic Facility Where Bitcoin Is Mined'. *Wired*, 3 November. Retrieved 19 August 2023 from https://www.wired.com/story/iceland-bitcoin-mining-gallery.

May, Timothy. 1988. 'The Crypto Anarchist Manifesto'. *Open Access Online*. Retrieved 19 August 2023 from https://nakamotoinstitute.org/crypto-anarchist-manifesto.

Nakamoto, Satoshi. 2008. 'Bitcoin: A Peer-to-Peer Electronic Cash System'. *Open Access Online*. Retrieved 19 August 2023 from https://bitcoin.org/bitcoin.pdf.

Rantala, Juho. 2019. 'Blockchain as a Medium for the Transindividual Collective'. *Culture, Theory, and Critique* 60(3–4): 1–14.

Russell, Stuart. 2022. 'Bitcoin 2022 Highlighted the Most Important Aspects of Bitcoin'. *Bitcoin Magazine*, 14 April. Retrieved 19 August 2023 from https://bitcoinmagazine.com/industry-events/bitcoin-2022-highlighted-aspects.

Schollmeier, Rüdiger. 2001. 'A Definition of Peer-to-Peer Networking for the Classification of Peer-to-Peer Architectures and Applications'. *Proceedings of the First International Conference on Peer-to-Peer Computing*, 101–2.

Singh, Munindar. 2001. 'Peering at Peer-to-Peer Computing'. *IEEE Internet Computing* 5(1): 4–5.

Stiegler, Bernard, and Irit Rogoff. 2010. 'Transindividuation'. *e-flux Journal*. Retrieved 19 August 2023 from https://www.e-flux.com/journal/14/61314/transindividuation.

Stiegler, Bernard, Ben Roberts, Jeremy Gilbert and Mark Hayward. 2012. 'A Rational Theory of Miracles: On Pharmacology, Transindividuation, an Interview with Bernard Stiegler'. *New Formations* 2012 (77): 164–84.

Swartz, Lana. 2018. 'What Was Bitcoin, What Will It Be? The Techno-economic Imaginaries of a New Money Technology'. *Cultural Studies* 32(4): 623–50.

———. 2021. 'Bitcoin as a Meme and a Future'. *Noema*, 11 February. Retrieved 19 August 2023 from https://www.noemamag.com/bitcoin-as-a-meme-and-a-future.

Zimmer, Zac. 2017. 'Bitcoin and Potosí Silver Historical Perspectives on Cryptocurrency'. *Technology and Culture* 58(2): 307–34.

Conclusion

Matan Shapiro

Cyclicity

Each chapter in this book explores heuristic concepts developed by cryptocurrency adopters, which inform diverse and at times even mutually exclusive analytic conclusions. While Cardoso argues that Bitcoin maximalists in Brazil conform to a *hyper-rationalized* socioeconomic and political discourse (which, following Golumbia (2018), he argues is fictional and dystopian), Vennonen, following Borch (2012) and Stage (2013), focuses on affective speech acts that constitute *phenomenological* reactions at a mass scale. Whereas Tuddenham conceptualizes individuation and communality on the blockchain as a *distinct form of transindividuation*, Tsavelis works with Ricoeur's (1980) narrative theory and Simmel's (2004) theory of money to claim that 'appification' encompasses both individualism and community to the extent they can be distinguished only as 'states of visibility'. Finally, Pickles challenges all the above by arguing that awareness to crowd behaviour among crypto bidders *annuls the subversive power of crowds*, which makes crypto prediction markets interchangeable with fiat prediction markets. Blockchain-mediated sociality emerges through all these perspectives as a multiscalar phenomenon, which at the level of collective organization turns on 'decentralizing' social institutions and at the level of individual action turns on the liberating potentiality of trustless technology.

In everyday life, these two levels of reference are connected in a cyclical and recursive rather than a dialectic fashion, continuously unfolding to produce crowds and infolding to demarcate communities. The arbitrary synchronization of individual decisions produces monetary values on the blockchain, whose pursuit en masse generates crowds, which are split into ad hoc localized communities that follow their own political, economic or moral logic, all of which always influence the actions and ideas held by individual members, whose synchronized decisions now reform new crowds, which separate into new communities, and so on. Cyclicality here substantiates an experiential individualism that is deliberately divorced from the scrutinizing power of the collective.

The formation of this type of individualism thereby yields new moral economies that inform the establishment of a social movement that is massive in its global scope, yet minute, vernacular and rooted in its localized manifestation, all the way down to the whims, desires and eccentricities of the individual subjects that are taken to be its central building blocks. The billionaire Elon Musk, for example, has singlehandedly caused colossal fluctuations in the entire cryptocurrency market by tweeting his support for or occasional sell-off of his Dogecoin and Bitcoin holdings (Barber 2021). A contingency across these localized and globalized scales, understood in this book as metamorphoses of social singularities and multiplicities, turns mundane praxis on the blockchain into a fascinating example of crowd morphology. Below I further explicate this analytical direction.

Plurality

A multiscalar cyclical dynamic of social formation in the world of cryptocurrency adopters primarily means that interactions online are radically pluralized. During my research in a Bitcoin social club in Tel Aviv, Israel (2017–19), I realized at some stage that most of my interlocutors managed and sustained many digital contact points and identity avatars. Beyond presence in the obvious 'lifestyle' platforms such as Facebook, Discord and Reddit, these included accounts used exclusively for financial or business objectives on LinkedIn, Slack, Instagram and Twitter. Of course, they would also maintain many accounts in cryptocurrency trading floors that were connected to several digital wallets, at times controlling dozens of such wallets at once. Dispersed digital footprints across platforms, each aimed at interacting digitally with different online crowds, were seen as essential not only for perfecting one's public profile online but also for securing one's financial future.

The logic that sustains this pluralization is partly pragmatic, but it is also rooted in the ideological rejection of a so-called 'centralized' economic system, wherein financial transactions are monitored by 'third parties' (e.g. banks and the state; cf. Greenfield 2018). Due to their intermediary role, regulatory institutions wield enormous economic and political power, which most of my interlocutors claimed is detrimental to individual freedoms. To fix this, they advocated a move to the direct exchange of money between individuals, which bypasses 'third parties' through the immanent automation of trust on the blockchain (Hayes 2019). Disintermediating economic relations at large was thus seen to actively increase the autonomy of individuals while also strengthening the establishment of egalitarian social arrangements at the level of grassroots organization (Swartz 2017).

The central idiom informing these ideas is the notion of 'peer', i.e. the person or machine standing behind a single transaction on the blockchain. Every peer can hold many different cryptocurrency wallets at once, each of them assigned with a unique address that serves to identify it. A peer can also be a *group*, if an arrangement is made for several people at once to own and operate one or more cryptocurrency wallets. A peer does not have a social life in the phenomenological sense – it is just a number on the blockchain that sends and receives money – but it does have a documented history of transactions, given that the blockchain registers and saves all the transactions ever made. A peer is therefore a flat social interface, a contact point manifesting in multiple digital forms, all of which serve to interact with others without requiring 'third-party' mediation. Bitcoin maximalists, such as those analysed by Campos Cardoso, commonly claim that mass adoption will necessarily facilitate collective social arrangements that favour the singular totality of each 'peer-to-peer' exchange relation.

While embracing this stance, even *fetishizing* disintermediation in 'peer' relationships, interlocutors in Tel Aviv nonetheless always also referred to themselves as an 'open-source community' (*kehilat kod patuah* in Hebrew), which had global and local attributions. At the global level, they saw themselves as members of a revolutionary global crowd, and at the local level, they saw themselves as activists in an intentional community of equals. They regularly organized workshops, drinking events, conferences, and other formal or informal meet-ups devoted to strengthening relationships between those who felt they belonged. Economic transactions between 'community members', they claimed, will *always* be the driving force of Bitcoin as a societal agent of change. It is a nominal communitarian solidarity – the insistence on using Bitcoin and 'believing' in its power – that determines the pluralistic rather than individualistic horizons of any 'peer-to-peer' transaction in this context (Shapiro 2022).

These heuristic views are interesting because they constitute a circular relationship between individual actions (exchanging Bitcoin) and collective boundaries (membership of a community). It is the many millions of individual transactions on the blockchain that frame the moral force of the local community, whose very existence in turn *challenges* the intuitive separation between individual decision making and collective social agreements. Individuals are disjoined from the authority of collective institutions, but they remain essential components in the collaborative project that they nonetheless continue to define in *collective* rather than entirely atomistic terms. A global social movement of Bitcoin followers thus becomes a mass of loosely interconnected individual actors who collaborate *despite* their narrow economic interests, while the local 'community' of die-hard supporters recursively concretizes these same interests as moral rather than exclusively financial (i.e. focused on 'freedom').

This can also be expressed analytically in crowd-theory terms (Canetti 1962). At the microlevel, the Israeli Bitcoiners I met can be seen as an association of friends who, like groups of demonstrators in a mass rally, walk together in the crowd. What they called an 'open-source community' is a semantic attempt to control crowd amorphism, a process of stabilization that they enshrined in rituals that included drinking nights, commemoration of Bitcoin-specific holidays (such as the annual Pizza Day), and the ongoing dissemination of their message during designated assemblies and lectures. At the macrolevel, if we imagine a bird's-eye view of the same rally, the Bitcoin global crowd includes a multitude of humans morphing through cyberspace and geospace, barely recognizable as individuals at all, unbound by any containing boundaries. At the heuristic level membership in the community *and* the crowd is equally important for the ontological sense of 'being' a Bitcoiner, in Israel and beyond.

Alterity

I suggest that the recursive metamorphoses between individuals, communities and crowds reflect a radical contemporary transformation of the dynamic of social alterity. There is a shift from *extrinsic* gaze on the other – which is defined by a distinction between an observer and the object of observation – to *intrinsic* experience of alterity within the self. On the one hand, this truly substantiates the metaphor of the network as an ontological part of the self, intraconnecting people from within themselves to create a sort of Deleuzian plane of immanence. On the other hand, this also fragments the social self, obscuring dispositions while slicing the 'peer' into multiple interfaces that connect 'it' with other 'peers'. The use of a plurality of avatars shifts the edge of social accountability from the substance of one's own personality – i.e. the culmination and accumulation of his or her life experiences and capabilities – away to the perceived impact of one's self-imposed masks on the structural context in which these masks are employed. There is a Goffmanian quality to this shift, which turns social life into a sliding stage, a constant reality show, which includes a strong commercial element.

Since Bitcoin (followed by many other decentralized assets) has come of age side by side with the emergence of interactive screens such as those on smartphones, smart TVs and VR glasses, it took the disruption of financial markets into wider realms of visual differentiation. The dominance of the selfie and its variants exemplify well how perspectival views of the self as a composite plurality spill over into the aesthetics of the body. Some time ago, for example, I was at a nightclub in London and saw a girl who suddenly discovered there was a huge wall mirror near the toilet area. She called her friends to join her, and they all posed in front of this mirror to take selfies. They stood in front of that mirror, which reflected their image, thus allowing them to look at themselves posing, while also reproducing that same image by photographing their image in the mirror. The final product, a photograph, contained the image of them looking at themselves in the mirror while picturing themselves doing this. Put simply, they were looking at themselves from the outside while they were also experiencing the power of the gaze inside. The point being that a selfie is not just an image you take of yourself, it is also a position in which you are simultaneously the observer and the object of observation. In selfies there is no simple or linear relationship between observers and observed, which as a determinant of the visibility of the other, further instantiates a recursive self-other dynamic in the pluralization of peer-to-peer exchange relations; even beyond the sphere of cryptonomics.

The Whole Earth Catalogue 1968 publication of a picture of Earth taken from an American space shuttle can be seen as the point of genesis of this dynamic. The picture represents humanity taking a picture of itself, generalizing itself, and in the realm of Stuart Brand's neoleftism, also advocating human unity.[1] The picture was stunning for those who saw it when it was published not just because of its historical value (i.e. the newly acquired ability of humankind to go outside of itself in a radical sense), but also because it exemplified the potential complementarity between objects and subjects. This was so because the picture effectively turns Planet Earth into a subjective being *as it is objectified from the outside*. The subjectivity of the planet is of course a matter of cultural interpretation, but it is a fact that precisely this direction was promoted by Brand and his collaborators (first in the Whole Earth Catalogue and later in *Wired* magazine), who sought to superimpose the very idea of 'humanity' with the image of a globe, a globality produced out of the fragility and primeval beauty of the planet (Turner 2006).

The idea that humanity and the globe represent one another is a radical development of Enlightenment dualist thought, which promoted an abstract concept of the human mind separated from and superior to ecological or geopolitical values. The selfie of Earth enabled the universalization of humanity not in abstract terms, but as a totalized whole that is at once spiritual and material. The immensity of the planet mirrors the vastness of the entire human race, which thus becomes a meta-crowd, i.e. a colossal human mass that encompasses diverse crowds within it; geographically, politically and morally. The selfie of Earth thus represented the planet-humanity as a multiplicity that is singular, a *monad* containing life while simultaneously also being a basic substance of life forms or systems (Latour et al. 2012). In the context of blockchain-mediated sociality, the strength of this image and its iconic status allude to the cyclical pluralization of the idiomatic mythology of 'freedom' (Faustino et al. 2022), which cryptocurrency adopters enhance both at the level of the individual (the exclusive ability to control funds) and the level of the collective (decentralizing institutions). In short, the monism of 1960s communalists gradually became integral to digitalization, a fact that inspired crypto adopters decades later to pluralize the experience of alterity as a property of encapsulated individuals.

Simultaneity

This monistic view is encoded in the functionality of blockchains. Take nonfungible tokens (NFTs) as a poignant example. Encrypted with a code that cannot be changed or hacked, NFTs are uniquely identifiable visual icons whose potential monetary value is derived from their singularity. Whether they are originally made in a digital form or from a picture of an actual object, makes no difference. Since it is encrypted, the representation has an exclusive stamp, like an immortal image frozen in time (e.g. the falling soldier from the Spanish Civil War or the napalm burnt girl in the Vietnam War). Each NFT is therefore an image or address – an object of gaze – *which is simultaneously subjective* due to its total uniqueness and rarity. In principle, this turns any NFT into a provisional observer (or an actor) that is looking back at us merely by proclaiming its original pedigree and aura (viz. Benjamin 1936). As with the selfie of Earth, the duplicity of the image as both observer and observed here generates a felt simultaneity, a ubiquitous experience of this duality, which annuls its internal contradictions.

This explicates why cryptocurrency adopters in Tel Aviv and beyond perceive the 'Fear of Missing Out' (cf. the chapters by Vennonen and Campos Cardoso in this volume) as an affective force that works both inside people and beyond them, circulating through one's own mind while at the same time spreading outwards to draw in vast crowds and thus influence decision making in the plural. As Tuddenham, Pickles and Tsavelis also emphasize in their respective contributions to this volume, adopters of cryptocurrency across the world consciously enhance both these types of affective flow, glorifying methodological individualism as the epitome of freedom while still advocating a collective cohesion rich in symbolic and moral content. Like Alice's bite of a cake in Wonderland, exchange on the blockchain serves to both expand and reduce imaginary social units, intermittently structuring 'individuals' (or 'peers'), 'communities' and massive global crowds in a dynamic of affective flow that unfolds and infolds recursively.

This process symmetrically requires a thorough reimagination of the configurations of singularities and multiplicities in blockchain-mediated sociality. If, as Elias Canetti (1962) claims, crowds crystallize when people 'lose their fear from being touched', attention to economic decentralization online must explicate the heuristic meaning of digital-economic 'touch'. If, as Christian Borch (2012) argues, semi-conscious suggestion is at the heart of the formation of economic trends online, an elaborate theory of affective contagion (Tarde 1903) on blockchains must come to the fore (Hayden 2021). And if, as cryptocurrency adopters themselves claim, 'belief' in the power of highly unstable decentralized markets is seen to liberate people from hegemonic economic and political structures – despite chaotic value fluctuations – scholars must rethink such concepts as 'the risk society' (Beck 1992) or 'rational individualism', which turn on the exact opposite stance, namely, that freedom equals predictability (cf. Pickles in this volume). Fresh insights on the simultaneity of affect and the recursive dynamic of value on the blockchain can thus inspire theoretical revisions even beyond the realm of economics.

Attention to these theoretical issues may also change the answers to empirical questions with which scholars have been grappling during the last decade, and that still incentivize further research on decentralized sociality: what are the processes and techniques that create crowds and communities on decentralized digital platforms beyond those mentioned in this volume? Which dynamics prevent blockchain crowds from congregating into smaller-scale, semi-enclosed communities? Which affective and structural processes impact the fragmentation of these communities (cf. Faria 2022)? And how are blockchain crowds and communities culturally shaped, socially accepted or contested, and politically legitimized or condemned through risk apprehension rather than aversion?

Crowds

This book demonstrates that decentralized forms of economic organization are no longer a negligible fringe phenomenon. Rather, they are social forms sustained by committed activists who see themselves as pioneering explorers of emergent new techno-utopian realities. What began in 2008 with a few cypherpunks committed to propagate the use of private money, transformed over the years into a massive social movement. This movement includes a strong collective aspect, often manifesting in the idea of a unified and egalitarian 'community', as well as a strong individualistic (and 'rational') element. The contributors have provided in their respective chapters highly original insights into the pulsating cyclical dynamic that is at the core of 'cryptonomic' praxis, which they theorize as a creative, motivating and fluid force in the forming of crypto crowds.

The analyses innovatively show, in different ways, that crowding on the blockchain not only causes a discharge of individual feelings of connectivity (Canetti 1962), but also awakens the attention of these individuals to the presence of others in cyberspace. This awareness can be rational and calculated – as Pickles, Campos Cardoso and Tsavelis demonstrate – but it can also be embodied or suggestive, as Vennonen and Tuddenham show. The morphology of crowd forming and unforming in blockchain-mediated sociality depends on processes of simultaneity, recursively and folding (viz. Handelman 2021), which influence the multiscalar dynamics of affective circulation on and increasingly also off the blockchain. By tracing this process empirically, it becomes possible to uncover the kinds of bridges (or tunnels) across the virtual and the actual, which emergent new forms of decentralized economic edgework (i.e. voluntary risk taking in markets) continuously produce.

This method might also be useful for the analysis of contemporary crowding phenomena beyond the sphere of cryptocurrency trading. Think, for example, of the forming of such recent social movements as MeToo and Black Lives Matter; in each case, concerted efforts to mobilize people online grew into a distinct global movement, which includes ideologically multifaceted and geographically dispersed local communities. These movements were restructured offline to maximize their respective political and juridical effects. Crowding, which is characterized by the simultaneous circulation of affects 'inside' and 'outside' people, should be taken seriously as a major contemporary societal force that participates in the constitution of diverse societal values (Borch and Knudsen 2013), whether these are monetary as in stock and crypto trading, aesthetic as with the role of selfies in new visibility regimes, or moral as with hashtags, memes and other viral instigators of public opinion (cf. Hayden 2021).

Masses that converge online for the pursuit and defence of diverse values thus prompt wider cultural transformations (Kapferer and Gold 2018), whose economic dimension is only secondary. Risk taking, a plurality of contact points with 'peers' and a monistic worldview, for example, are all elemental to emergent forms of sociodigital mobilization, which include such phenomena as the spread of conspiracy theories and the political weaponization of false/fake news. Like die-hard cryptocurrency supporters, people who consume/produce these forms of information on diverse kinds of media also antagonize established truths. Often they even defy the authority of previously trusted social institutions, instead forging new semantic and material connections between individual experience and the inundating power of the marching masses (cf. Borch and Knudsen 2013).

I hope that the methodological directions proposed in each of the chapters of this critical intervention, and the volume collectively, will encourage researchers interested in the contemporary digitalization and datafication of everyday life to further explore how constituent forms of power intersect with the organic implementation of techno-utopian collective arrangements, as well as the ways in which these empirical intersections are embedded in individual praxis, community formation and crowd dynamics.

Matan Shapiro is a social anthropologist currently researching synoptic surveillance and changing notions of alterity online as part of the European Research Council (ERC)-funded Surveillance and Moral Community (SAMCOM) Project at the department of Digital Humanities, King's College London.

Note

1. As I explained in the Introduction, Stewart Brand is a pioneering tech entrepreneur and the publisher of the *Whole Earth* magazine (cf. Turner 2006).

References

Barber, Gregory. 2021. 'When Musk Tweets about Crypto, It's Eloncoin All the Way Down'. *Wired*, 17 May. Retrieved 19 August 2023 from https://www.wired.com/story/elon-musk-dogecoin-bitcoin-tweets-price.

Beck, Ulrich. 1992. Risk Society: Towards a New Modernity, Mark Ritter (trans.). London: Sage.

Benjamin, Walter. 1936. 'The Work of Art in the Age of Mechanical Reproduction'. Retrieved 19 August 2023 from https://www.marxists.org/reference/subject/philosophy/works/ge/benjamin.htm.

Borch, Christian. 2012. *The Politics of Crowds: An Alternative History of Sociology*. Cambridge: Cambridge University Press.

Borch Christian, and Britta Knudsen. 2013. 'Postmodern Crowds: Reinventing Crowd Thinking'. *Distinktion: Scandinavian Journal of Social Theory* 14(2): 109–13. DOI:10.1080/1600910X.2013.821012.

Canetti, Elias. 1962. *Crowds and Power*. Trans. By Carol Stewart. Victor Gollancz: London.

Faria, Inês. 2022. 'When Tales of Money Fail: The Importance of Price, Trust, and Sociality for Cryptocurrency Users.' *Journal of Cultural Economy* 15(1): 81–92. Available online: https://doi.org/10.1080/17530350.2021.1974070.

Faustino, Sandra, Inês Faria and Rafael Marques. 2022. 'The Myths and Legends of King Satoshi and the Knights of Blockchain'. *Journal of Cultural Economy* 15(1): 67–80. DOI:10.1080/17530350.2021.1921830.

Golumbia, David. 2018. 'Zealots of the Blockchain'. *The Baffler*. Open Access online.. https://thebaffler.com/salvos/zealots-of-the-blockchain-golumbia (last accessed 29 September 2023).

Greenfield, Adam. 2018. *Radical Technologies: The Design of Everyday Life*. London: Verso.

Handelman, Don. 2021. 'Epilogue: Forming Form, Folding Time (toward Dynamics through an Anthropology of Form)', in Matan Shapiro and Jackie Feldman (eds), *Moebius Anthropology: Essays on the Forming of Form*. Oxford: Berghahn Books, pp. 289–345.

Hayden, Cori. 2021. 'From Connection to Contagion'. *Journal of the Royal Anthropological Institute* 27: 95–107.

Hayes, Adam. 2019. 'The Socio-technological Lives of Bitcoin'. *Theory, Culture & Society* 1–24. DOI:10.1177/0263276419826218.

Kapferer, Bruce, and Marina Gold. 2018. 'The Cuckoo in the Nest: Thoughts on Neoliberalism, Revaluations of Capital and the Emergence of the Corporate State, Part 1'. *Area Magazine* 151: 31–34.

Latour, Bruno, Pablo Jensen, Tommaso Venturini, Sébastien Grauwin and Dominique Boullier. 2012. '"The Whole Is Always Smaller Than Its Parts": A Digital Test of Gabriel Tardes' Monads'. *British Journal of Sociology* 63(4): 590–615.

Lee, Raymond L.M. 2017. 'Do Online Crowds Really Exist? Proximity, Connectivity and Collectivity'. *Distinktion: Journal of Social Theory* 18(1): 82–94. DOI:10.1080/1600910X.2016.1218903.

Ricoeur, Paul. 1980. 'Narrative Time'. *Critical Inquiry* 7(1): 169–90.

Shapiro, Matan. 2022. 'Crypto-egalitarian Life: Ideational and Materialist Approaches to Bitcoin'. *Social Analysis: The International Journal of Anthropology* 66(3): 62:82. DOI:10.3167/sa.2022.660304.

Simmel, Georg. 2004. *The Philosophy of Money*. London: Routledge.

Stage, Carsten. 2013. 'The Online Crowd: A Contradiction in Terms? On the Potentials of Gustave Le Bon's Crowd Psychology in an Analysis of Affective Blogging'. *Distinktion: Journal of Social Theory* 14(2): 211–26. DOI:10.1080/1600910X.2013.773261.

Swartz, Lana. 2017. 'What Was Bitcoin, What Will It Be? The Technoeconomic Imaginaries of a New Money Technology'. *Cultural Studies* 32(4): 623–50.

Tarde, Gabriel. 1903. *The Laws of Imitation*, Else Clews Parsons (trans.). New York: Henry Holt and Company.

Turner, Fred. 2006. *From Counterculture to Cyberculture: Stewart Brand, the Whole Earth Network, and the Rise of Digital Utopianism*. Chicago: University of Chicago Press.

www.ingramcontent.com/pod-product-compliance
Lightning Source LLC
Chambersburg PA
CBHW071713020426
42333CB00017B/2250